# Asum Grammar

## Selected articles of
## Ben Judd

## Acknowledgements

Ben Judd wrote his articles on 'Asum Grammar' for the *Evesham Journal* and I must, in the first instance, thank the *Journal* and its editor for granting permission to re-publish these articles.

The staff at Evesham Public Library has provided invaluable help and assistance, and I happily recommend their excellent local collection to anyone and everyone interested in local history.

Where an article was found in the back copies of the *Evesham Journal* held in the library, it appears with a date. Where an article was found elsewhere, then it appears without a date. If I have missed any articles, please do send me a copy and hopefully it will appear in a future revised version.

## Copyright

## Publisher

Vale of Evesham Historical Society
The Almonry Heritage Centre
Abbey Gate
Evesham
Worcestershire
WR11 4BG
United Kingdom

www.vehs.org.uk


December 2008

ISBN 978-0-9558487-1-1

# Introduction by Alistair McGowan

I must admit I haven't found it easy to describe the contents of this book. It's sort of self-explanatory and then... isn't !

As an ambassador to WWF-UK (part of the global World Wide Fund for Nature) and a campaigner on environmental issues, I wonder at the possibility of recycling. Rather than throwing out old words, shouldn't we be green and reduce rubbish by recycling them? After all, there's a lot of time-tested and quality Anglo-Saxon in here.

Imagine hearing '*Igertell*' and '*Yunnit*' peppered in conversation as you wander down the High Street on a Saturday morning. At the grocers how about ordering '*half a pound a them byuns there, an summa them paize!*' In the pub how would it feel to overhear: '*Iger tell if thee assn't bin drinkin my beer agyun. Woddus myun yourn? It yunt yourn, it's mine, mine tha, an it yunt beer it's jerkum. You bin in yur so long thee cossunt tell what's what, yur yud be right middlin, if thee knowest wot I myuns.*'

Makes you think, doesn't it? I mean, really, seriously, doesn't it make you think?

Beautifully observed, with Ben Judd's trademark tongue-in-cheek academia, these articles (which I remember fondly) attempt to explain and will hopefully help preserve our much-neglected Evesham accent. Part history, part grammar lesson and a whole lot of fun!

*[signature: Alistair McGowan]*

## A view of the Vale . . .
### . . . with Observer

"*Wur bist thee agooin'?*"
"*I byunt agooin' nowur.*"
"*Thee cossn't say that. Thee bist walkin' bisn't?*"
"*I be agooin' 'ome.*"
"*Why wasn't you at the do last noight? If I'd a knowed thee wasn't agooin' I 'ouldn't awent.*"
"*I went 'oomonin' in Asum.*"

How long is it since you heard this sort of conversation? Perhaps the young folk of today, educated largely by television talk, have never heard it.

Is the Asum, style of conversation dying out? If so, should an effort be made to preserve it, as ancient languages are kept alive by ardent societies?

Bill Clarke, a former *Journal* editor, kept Asum Grammer in mind by his witty extracts from a fictitious dictionary.

Someone suggested to me that a society should be formed to keep it alive. I suppose the members would greet each other with "*Ow bist?*" and carry on with such expressions as "*It's yuppust yut*" (half-past eight), "*Our Mam give me a good 'idin'*," and "*I yurd as old Bill be jud and 'is old 'oomon's bawling 'er yud off.*"

My grandmother quoted what she claimed she had heard shouted by a boy in the street. "*Thur's a foire at Cleeve Proire, one rick affoire and another boi 'er!*"

That's worth preserving. But is '*Igertell if it chunt*" and '*Wot supper thee? Got the collywobbles?*" worth recording for posterity?

Some anecdotes can only be told successfully in dialect. My old schoolmate Fred Archer knows this and his books are laced with them.

Fred still retains his Asum, accent and uses it to good effect in his talks.

I reckons I shall '*ave ter 'ave a goo one day.*

It'll certainly baffle the French.

# Foreword (or 'Preface' if you prefer)

Although the by-line Ben Judd appeared in the *Evesham Journal* on a mass of articles covering a wide range of subjects (including an interview with the Vale's one-time MP, Michael Spicer), his writings on the 'Asum Grammar' gained him a widespread and loyal following. However, the identity of Ben Judd remained a (moderately) well-kept secret for many years, only being publicly revealed much later as the pseudonym of Charles William Clarke, editor of the *Evesham Journal* from 1961 to 1983, who retired "to become a publisher. He is now a member of the firm of Ben Judd and Company..." (*Journal* 3/11/1983).

The name 'Ben Judd' was apparently intended as a pun on the pronunciation of 'Bengeworth' (a village officially incorporated into the Borough of Evesham in 1605). However, this pun wasn't as obvious as it might have been: my father (no doubt among others) thought it meant 'judd' (as in 'dead') a local word which in retrospect seems sadly and aptly descriptive of our slowly fading (faded?) local language.

On the basis that too much of a good thing can be, well, erm, simply too much, the articles on 'Asum Grammar' have been split into sections. In the pages in-between you will find odd snippets of Asum-as-she-wur-spoke, including poetic jottings from the letters page of the *Journal* and the pronunciation of place names.

Most articles have been (slowly) culled from backcopies (1950 to 1983) of the Vale of Evesham edition of the *Evesham Journal* held on microfiche at Evesham Public Library. Other ones (undated) are from the files of Gordon Alcock.

A while ago I worked in Malvern (distant enough to be foreign but not too foreign) and the wife of one of my colleagues worked in a Worcester health trust. Well, it seems that one of the many abbreviations then used by the doctors in Worcester was 'NFE': meaning 'Normal For Evesham.' I'm not sure what to make of this, but it tickles me still, and I can't help thinking that 'Asum Grammar' is a fine example of NFE.

In closing I should perhaps add that this is book to be dipped into, not raced through, a book to be savoured and considered. And that, I think, is enough introduction. Time to hand over to Ben Judd. *Yur thee bist, then.*

Stanley Brotherton
Bengeworth

The Bell Tower
Evesham ✠

# Names of Places

By way of a brief introduction, perhaps first we ought to run through the proper pronunciation of places in the Vale.

| Standard spelling | Proper pronunciation |
| --- | --- |
| Abbot's Lench | Hob Lench |
| Alcester | Awster |
| Ashton | Aishen |
| Bengeworth | Benjuth or Ben-jud |
| Bishampton | Bissapp'n |
| Bricklehampton | Brick-lund or Bickledun |
| Broadway | Broady |
| Campden | Camdin |
| Cerney | Sawney |
| Charlton | Chol-ton |
| Comberton | Cummerton |
| Cropthorne | Crapton |
| Dormstone | Darms'n |
| Ebrington | Yubbert'n |
| Elmley | Embley |
| Evesham | A-sum |
| Gotherington | Guthert'n |
| Grafton | Graf'n (short a) |
| Honeybourne | Honey-bun |
| Inkberrow | Ink-bru |
| Kersoe | Kessa |
| Kington | Kyine |
| Marston | Maas'n (short a) |
| Naunton Beauchamp | Naun, also Dirty Naun |

| Standard spelling | Proper pronunciation |
|---|---|
| Offenham | Uffenum |
| Pebworth | Pebbuth |
| Pershore | Persha, or Pawsha* |
| Stanway | Stanny |
| Stoulton | Stout'n |
| Swinesherd | Swenshud |
| Throckmorton | Frogmort'n |
| Upton Snodsbury | Upton Snadgbury |
| Wickham | Weekun |

And now for some places a little further afield:

| Standard spelling | Proper pronunciation |
|---|---|
| Alve-church | All-church |
| Birmingham | Brummijum |
| Kidderminster | Kiddy-mister |
| Madresfield | Match-field |
| Malvern | Mawvun |
| Powick | Pwoyk |
| Severn | Sivvun |
| Smethwick | Smerrick |
| West Bromwich | West Brummidge |
| Whittington | Wittenton |
| Worcester | Ooster |

---

* In a good year, it's *Persha, where d'ya think*, in a bad year *Persha, God help us.*

# More 'Asum Grammar'

## More 'Asum Grammar' (28<sup>th</sup> April 1956)

In deference to the wishes of innumerable readers and at fantastic trouble and expense, we are able to present here a few more short extracts from that learned work, long in preparation, upon the fascinating but difficult subject of 'Asum Grammar.' But first we are strictly enjoined by the compiler to point out on thing especially which he considers to be extremely important yet which may easily be misunderstood by the casual reader if it be not made crystal clear.

In beginning his task, the compiler did not see his enterprise as a joke but rather as a serious effort to save a little bit of old England from spoliation by the unworthy. Himself taught to sound his aitches and conjugate his verbs with utmost propriety (though born, bred and partly educated in the town of his forefathers) he does not always say *thee bist* himself but will be the last man in the town to make fun of those who do; and, to go further, he will be the first to raise the standard in their defence.

His 'Asum Grammar' is intended to do for the Evesham language what the late Mr. Fowler did for the parent tongue in the matter of usage: to stop the rot before it were too late and to insist on purity without pedantry. Here goes, then.

> **ASS** – short for *hast*. Example, *ass thee sin that old ummun wot yuts pigs' fit for er tay?* This is the interrogative form. As a categorical statement, it becomes: *theets sin that old ummun,* etc… which is, grammatically, a very interesting phenomenon indeed.

> **FUST** – first. Example: *thee bissn't the fust erv ad, an er'll av tha agyun, if thee knowest wot I myuns.*

> **ERV** – 3<sup>rd</sup> per. sing. (fem only) pres. indic., verb "to have." Example: *erv sin tha.* Note, that the word "she" does not appear in the Evesham language, except perhaps very occasionally among those who still keep pigs.

## More pages from the 'Asum Grammar' (16<sup>th</sup> June 1956)

In no wise are the power and resilience of the Evesham language more aptly to be demonstrated than in the use of the expression *theest* and *theets*. Indeed, it has been most delicately argued in more reputable places that this that people born south of Hinton Cross, north of the Wheelbarrow and Castle, west of the

New Inn at Cropthorne or east of Mickleton Tunnel can never master it, even with the help of highly paid tutors. But in this there may be some exaggeration. Yet hope springs eternal in the human breast, and not without reason: we are reliably informed that a long essay exploring the ramifications of *theest* and *theets* will appear in volume III of that learned work, long in preparation but still avidly awaited, the 'Asum Grammar.' This is excellent news. More happily still, we are enabled by kind permission of the compiler to present a short extract here, where (as you ought to know by now) those in need of enlightenment may sometimes pick up little pearls of truth. The copyright is strictly reserved, of course.

*Theest* and *theets* equally belong to all the verbs in the Evesham language, always in the second person singular and more frequently and effectively in the passive than the active voice; but they are distinguished by their tenses. In the present indicative there is only *theest* in its simplest, purest form – in which it is always followed by that rather Germanic-sounding encumbrance, *got*. For example: *Theest got a fly in thee eye. Theest got a good patch a onions thur, you.* (In passing, pray note that *you* is the vocative case form of *thee* when the latter is exclusively a nominative and it has no other function whatsoever: it is an exquisite grammatical jewel which needs a far larger setting than it is going to get here and now on this humble occasion; but its turn will come, never fear). *Well, theest got it now, assn't?*

Let us pass to the distinctions, then. One may say that *theest* is Perfect and *theets* is Pluperfect, in either the indicative or the subjunctive mood, although this still leaves a great deal unsaid. In volume IX, appendix F, pp.401 *et seq.*, the examples include the following:

> **Perfect**: *Theest bin drinking that scrumpy agyun, er sez. Theest yerd wot er said, assn't? Theest made a bit on them cabbages, I know.*

> **Pluperfect**: *Theets ad enough a that scrumpy afore I come, you. Woddus myun? When I see that jarrin to the vicar last Sunday atternun theets got a drop on tha, addnst? Thee dussenarf look middlin, you, as if theets swallud a pill as didn't suit tha.*

Yes – you will have seen that it leaves far too much unsaid. Unsuccessful attempts at over-simplification are one of the curses of modern life, as all readers of newspapers should know to their cost. There remains hardly any space for examples of two other usages of *theets*. We think they are two, and not one. First: *Theets take that wench down th' Oxstalls meddas if erd goo a tha, uddenst?* Second: *Aye, and theets sun be in trouble if er told er old man about tha, shouldnst?* This is all for the present.

Seasoned old temperance campaigners may object that there is too much wine, women and song in the 'Asum Grammar.' If so, we regret that we cannot help it. In the first place, O gentle, withdrawn, inhibited readers, we did not write the book or invent the quotations that have been presented here, so it is beyond our control. In the second place, that is life, dear friends, that is life.

# 'Asum Grammar' (20<sup>th</sup> July 1956)

Browsing through the three volumes devoted to adverbs in that learned work, so long in preparation, the 'Asum Grammar,' one cannot help noting the superior ***musicality*** of our native words and phrases. Ideally, one feels, this monumental work should be presented to the world not in book form, as the compiler contemplates, but on discs or tape: so that the metrical purity of fine cadences can be preserved. English orthography, as you will remember with sorrow from your childhood, is a completely crooked business; and so chancy, too. Adverbs, one might think, are of no great help to the poet in a country where the ending –ly is suppressed from all but the adjective *lovely* and a few weak companions. Yet ready-made conclusions, as we have told you before, will not fit the Evesham language.

*Yur thee bist. Thur ee goos agyun.* Can you conceive of more euphonious sentences than these, streams of speech more pleasant to the human ear, sounds more luminescent? Undoubtedly not, unless you are Dante. But observe, if you please, that the poetic quality springs in each case from the adverb. This is astonishing but it is nevertheless true. In volume VII, pp.252 *et seq.*, there is an appendix which is notable for no other reason than because all its forty five pages are filled with examples indicating the proper use of three, a mere three, adverbs. With the kind permission of the compiler we are enabled to present a short selection here.

> *Don't thee forget I'm yur and I can yur tha, thee knowst.*
>
> *Wur dust thee set when thee cumst yur?*
>
> *I sets anywur I likes, you.*
>
> *Theest bin a cummin yur a long time, assn't?*
>
> *Aye, I allus a come yur.*
>
> *Does thy old ummun come yur utha?*
>
> *No, a course er don't: er a gone down thur, you.*
>
> *Down wur?*
>
> *Down thur! Thee knowst wur down thur is, dussunt?*
>
> *Er yunt! Er ant gone down thur, av er?*
>
> *Well, wur dust thee think er a gone, you? Er yunt up yur – so er must be down thur.*

# More 'Asum Grammar' (5<sup>th</sup> October 1956)

In Boots the other day, a young man, anxious to engage the attention of one of those glamorous assistants of theirs, was pretending to buy a packet of razor blades, which she could see he was barely old enough to need. "No thanks, not theyrn," he repeated, wishing she would put the inconsequential things away and talk about something sweeter. So it continued for a little while, then "Oh!," she exclaimed, lacerating him with her lovely eyelashes, "I do wish you'd make up your mind – and talk English!"

This rebuff, as well as an overwhelming clamour on the part of innumerable scholars, compels us to dip again into the volumes of that learned work, long in preparation, the 'Asum Grammar,' in order that errors may be refuted and plain usage made plainer still. *Yur we guz agyun.*

In volume IV, pp.192-406, there is an exhaustive account, illustrated by many examples from modern usage, of the possessive and reflexive pronouns. The complete set of the 'Grammar' is worth its price on the merits of this section alone, as they will know who search this page for its occasional little pearls of truth, for whose benefit the compiler of the work has enabled us to reproduce a few examples below.

But it was an Absolute Possessive (volume X, appendix 3) that was smothered in scorn across that razor blade counter. *Theyrn.* There is nothing wrong with *theyrn.* There is nothing wrong with *isn* and *ern* and *ourn* and *yourn,* either. Some authorities, more interested in the origins that the usage of words, would have us believe that *theyrn* was once "their one" or "their own" and it may well have been so. The point is one of passing historical interest but otherwise unimportant as long as one avoids the error of inserting an intermediate trill. For example:

> *That car they be a getting in yunt theyrn, thee knowest: it's ourn.*

But it would be an error in Evesham to say, "their-un" and "our-un," which usage are alien and unworthy; yet, in sorrow, we have heard small boys mouthing them under our windows on their way along Swan-lane.

> *Giss summer them conkers them kids down thur githa, ut?*

> *What kids? Waddus myun? Them conkers wasn't "their-uns"; they'd only borrud um, thee knowst.*

Now this is grotesque. We should have thought that with all the millions poured into education, and the rates being what they are, to say nothing of the infinite holidays an indulgent state bestows on teachers – we should have thought, we repeat, that grammatical blunders of this kind were impossible.

"Their-un," of course, is an alien substitute, something like "they'm" for "they be," and it belongs not to Evesham but to the vast industrial area which lies to the north of Bidford-on-Avon. How much truer and more nobly ring *theyrn* and *ourn*.

> *Thy telly's bigger than ourn, yunnit?*

> *Aye, I specso, but it churn arfus big as theyrn down thur, mine tha!*

There is much more to say about isn and ern. For the present, however, there is barely space left for a tiny illustration. *Er a got isn in a locket round er neck but er dunno wur e got ern. Do er?*

# More 'Asum Grammar' (16th November 1956)

"Come, lasses and lads! Get leave of your dads! And away to the maypole, hie!" The people of Evesham know the tune quite well: a jolly, galloping tune, fit for marching soldiers: it is played on the second barrel of the Bell Tower carillon several times *per diem*. And *per noctem*, too: a sore trial for certain dads. But here we shall concern ourselves only with the words, or, rather, with one word in particular: lasses. According to that learned work, long in preparation but still eagerly awaited, the 'Asum Grammar,' there is no such word as lass. It should be wench.

Through the liberality of the compiler, who permits us to browse through the manuscript from time to time, we are here enabled to present a few extracts from the long article about Wenches, which appears in volume X, pp.200-350. This article is not only vast in its scope and profound in its judgements but is illustrated into the bargain, which is a great deal more than can be said for anything in the Shorter Oxford Dictionary, price 5gns. Clearly it is real value for money. *Yur thee bist, then.*

*Lass* means "A girl (not much used in the south)." Its etymological derivation has to be compared with the Middle Swedish *lösk kona*, which is hardly surprising when you come to think of it. Wench means "A girl, maid, young woman," and is derived from the Old English *wencel* through the Early Middle English *wenchel*, of which the Middle English *wenche* is a shortened form. *Thee bist my wench* is a good example. The language of courtship does not always reach such pinnacles of pure poetry. *Ers is wench, not thine. I a got three wenches at wum. Ers a lovely little wench, yunner?*

"Prythee how many Boyes and Wenches must I haue?" wrote Shakespeare, and he knew the language, if anybody did. Pray note that he did not refer to lasses and lads. The same author, it must be admitted, did, on one occasion, see fit to write "It was a Louer and his lasse." But there were extenuating circumstances for this. For one thing, not even the Bard could manage to rhyme wench with grass and he was probably either too drunk at the time to have sat her on a bench, or there was only grass to sit on. These are things which every louer knows.

# More 'Asum Grammar' (11<sup>th</sup> January 1957)

The persistent clamour of scholars, rather than a lack of other subjects for dispute, causes the appearance here this week of further extracts from that learned work, overlong in preparation, overdue in publication, the 'Asum Grammar.' It is a clamour which shall not be denied.

As the late Mr. Fowler said, "the better the writer, the shorter his words." What holds good in the matter of English usage holds good equally in the spoken Asum language, which also is a living thing, flexible and adaptable, and most powerfully to be used in short bits.

*Yur thee bist, then*: a few short extracts from footnotes chosen here and there, beginning with the ants and the bees – the etymological, not entomological, kinds.

> **ANT.** 1<sup>st</sup> and 3<sup>rd</sup> pers. sing. 1<sup>st</sup>, 2<sup>nd</sup> and 3<sup>rd</sup> pers. pl., pres. indic. etc., negative form, verb "to have." The 2<sup>nd</sup> pers. sing. is assunt. Examples: *I ant sinner lately, nor thee assunt. Er ant ad none. Eee ant got none. We ant got none. You ant got none. They ant gone wum.*

> **BEE.** 1<sup>st</sup> and 3<sup>rd</sup> pers. sing., 1<sup>st</sup>, 2<sup>nd</sup> and 3<sup>rd</sup> pers. pl., pres. indic., etc., verb "to be." The 2<sup>nd</sup> pers. sing. is *bist* (cf. the German *du bist*, which strongly indicates to those who wonder about such things, that our ancestors were pig-headed Saxons like ourselves: the theory is developed, with illustrations in line and colour, in the long essay† "Saxon Survivals," vol. VII, pp.250-301.) Examples of bees: *I be better lookin un thee, yunt I? We be chargin 3d. fer this. You be thinking it chunt worth it. They be getting thee fourpences though. Yunt they?*

Now a word or two for more serious students of language, who are able to be distinguished from the mere seekers after little titters. The latter laugh superiorly at what they think, in their ignorance, to be a rustic dialect: the former know it to be nothing of the sort and laugh not at all, which is very short-sighted of them.

Yet the longer one ponders certain of the common Asum expressions, the faster one is dragged to this conviction: that the language is unique and incomparable, quite unlike any of the known urban or rural dialects of England. Most dialects depend for their surviving interest on thoroughly ungrammatical archaisms whose origins may only be found in the poor man's imitation of the rich man's speech. In Asum, there was never an aristocracy, so there was nothing to imitate and the language has remained a language. Consider these three euphonious old terms:

---

† And in any case, there is enough history on this page already. Ben Judd.

> **EARL**. *Earl see tha cummin, you. Then earl a tha.*
>
> **WORSE**. *Worst bin, ummun? Tell us, ut, worse bin?*
>
> **DUST**. *Dust the know earl tell im wur theest bin?*

# More 'Asum Grammar' (15<sup>th</sup> February 1957)

One of the Sunday newspapers, which is noted as much for its respectability as for sparing no expense to get to the bottom of things, is publishing a series of articles entitled "The Great Mystery." Each contribution relates an important person's belief about the life hereafter. Each draws many letters from readers. These are troubled times, indeed. We are not to be outdone. If it's theology you want, you have only to say the word and out it shall pour, in buckets full – real, full-bodied, rich stuff, and none of your half-measures.

But, in the meanwhile, it behoves a country newspaper such as this one to consider the specifically local aspects of great matters. It has been done before and it will be done again... Take, for an example, this matter of man's belief in the life hereafter.

Any attempt to throw light on the local aspects of a subject so majestic and profound might seem ridiculous – if not obscene. But it is ont entirely so, as we have recently discovered. In the 'Asum Grammar,' that learned work so long in preparation, so laggardly in publication, there is a discourse upon the morphology and semantics of a combination which is familiar to all who are well acquainted with the Evesham language. *Iger tell*.

Almost any attempt to analyse it in translation – that is, by pretending to find an exact Queen's English equivalent and applying the ordinary rules of grammatical analysis to that translation – leads into a quagmire. The combination is untranslatable.

> *Er said thee cossunt come wun a ma no mower. Iger tell.*
>
> *Eee yunt cummin because ee ant got no petrol. Iger tell.*
>
> *Ast thee yurd what that old ummun's bin jarrin about, you? Iger tell if it chunt thee er's bin a jarrin about, you. Iger tell.*
>
> *Bist thee gunner pick any mower sprouts this wik? Iger tell if I be.*
>
> *They said it was a gunner rain agyun all this wik but iger tell is the sun yunner gunner shine this atternun.*

To analyse the untranslatable is a rather tall order but the attempt must be made, or the Evesham might as well be dismissed as gibberish, or mumbo-jumbo.

> *And iger tell if it is. Iger tell if I sin tha. Iger tell if er ant done it agyun.*

The predicate is *ger*, the subject is *I* and the object is *tell* – that is, if *iger tell* is a simple sentence, complete. Some examples suggest that the construction may be optative but the compiler of the 'Asum Grammar,' by whose kind permission we are enabled to publish these occasional extracts from his monumental work, doubts if it can be so. In the sixth appendix to volume I (pp.350-382), he begins to explain why.

It is unreasonable to assume that an Evesham man is exercising willpower or expressing an intention when he says *iger tell*. His intention is simply to express surprise, astonishment or wonder; he finds the term useful when he wishes to indicate his regret at some slight disappointment or his complaint about an uncongenial circumstance.

*Iger tell if the assn't bin drinkin my beer agyun.* No Evesham man ever intended to hazard his salvation when he used such an expression as this. What he meant was simple enough. *Theest bin drinkin my beer agyun. Iger tell!* Rather like my brew of beer, my choice of heaven or hell is entirely my own and it depends on the will.

And there is the cause of the analytical difficulty: an uncertainty about the tense of *iger*. The first person singular in the future simple tense requires *shall* not *will*, unless a conscious exercise of the will is to be explicit. It is doubtful if Lucifer himself was ever capable' of that, according to the leading authorities.

So let us suppose the combination to be interrogative, perhaps in a defective form. *(Ull)iger tell?* Is this the voice of the tremulous conscience of Evesham Man? We do not think so. And besides, as Mr. Nesfield says:

> …in interrogative sentences, *will* is not used in the first person, for the obvious reason that it would be absurd for a man to question himself about his own intentions. (*Errors*, 1<sup>st</sup> edition, p.88)

Experiments suggest that this fascinating little fragment of our language may have fallen in one of those no man's lands which were explored by Mr. Fowler (*Modern English Usage*, 3<sup>rd</sup> edition, p.528):

> In clauses of indefinite future time, and indefinite relative clauses in future time, will is entirely unidiomatic; either shall is used, chiefly in formal contexts, or, much more often, futurity is allowed to be inferred from the context and a present is used.

Mr. Fowler, of course, did not mention *iger tell* in particular. But, undoubtedly, it is a question of an indefinite future time when a man, even an Evesham man, refers to the life hereafter.

*Iger tell.* We have seen that there is no *shall* to be found in *iger* and that there can hardly be a *will*. And so, unless the term we are discussing it to take its place with Mr. Fowler's 'time honoured' "I will be drowned, no-one shall save me!" (*Ibid*), as being much too good to be true, we are left with the present. And so it may be in eternity.

*Iger tell if it's a gunner whack ma, though.* The term as expressed thus is a future simple, if ever one was. *Iger tell if er didn't yut the lot.* Here is another Evesham usage but it is not identical, for if this *iger tell* be in the future the rest of the sentence must be nonsense. *Er's already yut the lot.* There are no ifs about it, and the journey from which there can be no return is quite unnecessary.

Readers will be now have suspected what the compiler of the 'Asum Grammar' has long been convinced of: that the ordinary rules and conventions by which the Queen's English is bound cannot constrain this language of ours. This is not to say that the Evesham language is chaotic or haphazard in either grammar or usage: in fact, the reverse is true: the forms authorised by tradition are so rigidly ordered that a speaker taking even the slightest liberty with an idiom brands himself as foreign to that place. Thus it is that the Evesham language maintains its unity and its purity undiluted and unsullied by the great social changes of the ages. It is a great thing to have survived so many revolutions and still be strong. *Well iger tell.*

THE GATEHOUSE AND ALMONRY

# More 'Asum Grammar' (12<sup>th</sup> April 1957)

Are they cruel to birds in Devon? The question occurred to us the other day after hearing again that well known song:

> Wur by yon blackbird to?
> Us know wur ee be:
> Ee be in yon turnup field,
> And us be atter ee.

It seems unlikely that those mellow-throated people, who address even complete strangers as "m'dear," can be unfriendly to such an innocent creature as the blackbird – which, in any case, is one of the protected species. So what is the purpose of the song?

Fortunately we have been able to delve recently into that learned work, long in preparation, but still unpublished, the 'Asum Grammar.' And in the section devoted to Comparative Philology (vol. IX, pp.1-236) we find this pregnant quotation, at p.89:

> *Wur bist thee gone, you?*
> *I knows wur thee bist:*
> *Thee bist us that opple tree,*
> *A-waitin thur fer me.*

This compiler then contrasts this with the Devonshire song already quoted and says:

> They both exist purely for the purpose of indicating correct usage: they are mnemonics: the blackbird's function is entirely orthoepic.

What strikes us as more interesting, to be frank, is the "turnup": that unfortunate vegetable the squires used to crush the peasants with (*Vide* E.W. Martin, "The Secret People"). But here we intend only to comment on the purity of the Evesham language, compared with the Devon dialect, where number is concerned. An Evesham man would never say "Us know" but *I knows* or, to continue the conjugation, *Thee knowst, Ee knows*, etc.

Moreover, he knows the difference between the subject and the object as well. He would never say, "Us be atter ee." Unfailingly, he would always say, with relentless decision, *We be atter im*. Or *we wuz*, or course. The Evesham man keeps his verbs in their place, also.

To return to the song, it seems likely that by such means tradition may keep an old language alive, because the words can be pronounced in one way only and no room is left for academic doubt.

By more difficult methods has the learned lady of Girton tried to re-incarnate the voice of Langland in her Third Programme version of "Piers Plowman." And we wish her the best of luck, for the job must be purgatorial. Worse that trying to write correct Evesham speech, using only the printable words.

# More 'Asum Grammar' (10<sup>th</sup> May 1957)

Never trouble yourself with trouble till trouble troubles you. As a proverb, it is like its brothers and sisters: crystal-clear at the first glance but naughtily equivocal at the second. The word "trouble" is worthy of appreciation, though: it is a versatile word, functioning in this short example alone as two kinds of verb and appearing, as a noun, in both the subject and the object.

Not only in the Queen's English, which gives the word a very respectable etymology, but in the Evesham language itself is there plenty of "trouble." The 'Asum Grammar,' that learned work long in preparation but still unpublished, contains numerous examples from life, some illustrated in colour and others in line, of the true uses of "trouble." *Yur thee bist, then*; but pray do not take it for granted or titter in the wrong places, for the expense is enormous, my friends.

"Trouble" came to the Evesham language in the Middle English period as an adaptation from the Old French and boasting itself a regular phonetic descendant from the Late Latin *turbulare* which means, roughly, to stir it up. It is not among the oldest of our words, such as the short and strong Saxon ones you are so fond of, but it is very expressive. It tends to be a word of the intellect rather than the emotions. For example: *Don't thee trouble thee yud about er* might be wise enough advice to a young man crossed in love; though it would be unlikely to succeed if his heart, not his head, were troubled.

When *trouble* is used as a verb in the Evesham language, there is nearly always a *yud* somewhere at hand, even if it is often merely understood. *Er teld im ta trouble is yud uv is own business* is a fairly common example still in popular use. It is understood to have been employed considerably in recent weeks during the local election campaigns but it is a long time since a policeman quoted it in court as a defendant's alleged reply to the charge.

*Thee trouble thee yud a thee own business and tell thy super I don't want trouble what ee sez.* They train young policemen very thoroughly nowadays but they do not yet teach the Evesham language at Hindlip and this defect, which ought to be remedied, is probably why court statements seem so unlikely in their phraseology.

*I don't trouble what thy super sez. Trouble* without the *yud* is capable of many uses, of which the last-quoted example is only one. It can be conjugated simply:

> *I don't trouble*
> *Thee dussunt trouble.*
> *Ee don't trouble*

...and so on. Or it can be developed: *I yunt gunner trouble...* and so on. So much for the verb, transitive and intransitive. The Evesham language shares also with the Queen's English the eleven approved uses of the word as a noun, including those concerned with unpleasant relations with the authorities and with the unfortunate unmarried woman's condition. But we need not trouble our *yuds* about *er*. *Er sez er yunt troubling er yud about nothing*. And there's defiance for you.

# More 'Asum Grammar' (7<sup>th</sup> June 1957)

Why, but why? It is a burning question. It has been touched upon before in these extracts from that learned work, long in preparation but still unpublished, the 'Asum Grammar,' and it will probably be touched upon again; for it is of compelling interest.

*Yur thee bist, then.* It is obvious enough, is it not, that the nose of that adverb is not a consonant but all that remains of a long, lost vowel, sounded for effect in the absence of the aspirate. *Eee-yur thee bist, if thee wanst it plainer*.

But in volume III, appendix D, of the 'Asum Grammar,' the compiler casts doubt on the reliability of this explanation in use as a general rule, and he especially refers to *yunt*, which is the negative form of the verb "to be" in the second person singular and plural, all genders:

| | |
|---|---|
| *Ee yunt* | *It yunt* |
| *Er yunt* | *They yunt* |

And, more profoundly different (though this is dealt with comprehensively in a long footnote, for it is not all that it seems), the interrogative form *yunnum*. *Them paze a thine yunt dooin very well, you. Yunnum?*

Now it would be too facile and also rather silly to suggest that there is an exact equivalent for *yunt* in "ain't," which was the Queen's English until long after Englishmen began to be educated by compulsion. *Yunt* is not "ain't." In fact, *it chunt nothin of the sort, you*.

Exhaustive research at vast expense has revealed that the Evesham *yunt* is derived immediately from the Cotswold *byunt*, which is of an identical origin etymologically. In Campden, there are still those who say *ee byunt*, instead of *ee yunt*, and one is compelled to ask, "Which came first?" not "Which sounds better?" to which latter question the answer is blatantly plain.

Which came first? Be assured, patient readers, the matter is in not doubt: the Evesham language acquired some of its words from the Hills but modified them, purified them if you like, as they descended into the Valley. So it is especially with *yunt* and *byunt*.

But always have caution, my friends: do not connect *byunt* with the stage rustic *baint*; for etymology is a much more exact science than that. For one thing, it is worth while considering why the fortunate people of Campden call that place Cyamdin (We refer to the genuine Cyamdin folk, not the imports of the Motor Age).

Why, but why? It is no easier to say. It is not the sort of contraction one could attribute to leisureliness of speech as, for example, is the apparent inclination of Broadway people to call their village Brordy. There is more to it than meets the eye. You will find, by and large, that the Evesham language is shorter in its treatment of vowels than the Cotswold language. You might have "pigs' fate" for your supper in Blockley, but in Evesham you would have *pigs' fit*. To be exact, which is the function of a grammarian if it can be achieved (though Heaven knows it is no simple matter), you would *yut pigs' fit*. Why, but why? *Funny, yunnit?*

# More 'Asum Grammar' (5<sup>th</sup> July 1957)

Summer, of a quality our elders remember, with benevolence from their youth, has been a long time *i-cumin* but now it is come and some of them are not satisfied even now. In Evesham on Sunday, a middle-aged woman complained: "*Yunnit ot!*" she said. O my friends! the things we take for granted... The perspiration of the moment will soon pass and will be forgotten. But the aspiration passed a long time ago and nobody knows where it went. *Yunnit ot!*

You may look in vain for it in the Shorter Oxford Dictionary, at five guineas a time. In Old English, it says, *h* occurred not only before the vowels but also before the consonants *l*, *n*, *r*, and *w*; it dates the first application of the Greek *spiritus asper* to the letter *h* in 1725; and deals much with the Middle English *ache*, which concerns us here not at all, especially today. Other works rate *h* a Scottish or a German thing, and then a guttural or a spirant.

To be honest, one learns but little more by referring to that learned work, long in preparation but still unpublished, the 'Asum Grammar.' The use and abuse of the aspirate in the Evesham language is described in volume III, appendix 5, pp.276-291. As you have probably guessed, it is mostly abuse, as the following short extracts indicate.

> One searches in vain for true aspirates in the Evesham language: the species on finds, as in the emphatic Greenhill, are all spurious, late nineteenth century accretions of the genteel classes, and all belong in any case to proper nouns.

*Yunnit ot!* though... is it a satisfactory exercise of language? Can it, in other words, be improved? Let us put that *h* in and try it again... "Yunnit hot!" *O tempora!* O secondary modern! O Birming*h*am!

In *Unnybun*, on the other hand, there never was an aspirate in living memory and the question to be asked is whether there was ever one at all, anywhere in this outlying island of the West which is called the Vale of Evesham.

Experiment suggests that there was; though it may not have been the orthoepic sort compelled in phrases like: "On yon high eastern hill." Middle English texts contains aspirates, and of a kind which call out to be pronounced – but very gently with a soft breath, just enough to separate the vowel from the consonant preceding. Modern Evesham texts ignore them altogether or, exceptionally, convert them to *y* or *w*. The appendix we have referred to gives the list of exceptions.

**YUR**. Hear, here. Examples: *Didst thee yur uz er was yur agyun? Ers bin yur, thur un everywur for donkey's ears, you.*

**YUD**. Head. Examples: *Thee trouble thee yud a thee own business. Ee fell yud fust.*

**YUP**. Heap. Examples: *I a bin through a yup a dictionaries fer this un, you. I'll see tha by the muck yup* (Note – A virtually untouched Anglo-Saxon survival. Our ancestors knew the word well but they did not say "heap." They probably had no diphone but emphasised the short a, which brought them very quickly to the yup. 'Gee-up' becomes *jup* in the same way.)

**WUM**. Home. Example: *Now I'm a-gooin wum.*

# More 'Asum Grammar' (9<sup>th</sup> August 1957)

*Thee shudst a-yurd um a-cussin!* The exclamation, voiced by a man in the Trade, was in no way surprising. For it is no pleasanter in the Vale of Evesham than it is elsewhere to be marooned by a thunderstorm. On licensed premises. After closing time.

Let us, my friends, take the *cussin* for granted as an expression of outraged human nature. But as an example of orthoepic usage it has more to it than meets the eye. Like Lord Beaverbrook's prose style. Shall we look a little closer at *cussin*? In the 'Asum Grammar,' that learned work long in preparation but still unpublished, the verb *cuss* is conjugated enormously, for it has many pitfalls. But it is in the section dealing with Omitted Consonants (volume V, pp.300-427) that we find *cuss* with all its seven companions: *fust, fuzz, dust, nuss, puss, vuss* and *wuss*. And what an interesting lot they are...

The Evesham language is not alone in dropping the *r* from curse: tinkers' cusses are cheaper than ten a penny anywhere in England and way back in the wild and woolly West the natives find their chief enjoyment a-feudin and a-cussin, as everybody knows. And naturally enough: worthless consonants may as well be dropped and there is none less valuable than *r* when it appears between *i* or *u* and *s*. Consider the examples:

**CUSS, etc**     *Thee shudst a-yurd um a-cussin. Er wunnarf cuss tha. Oo bist thee a-cussin?*

**FUST**     *Fust come, fust served. Ee went yud fust. Thee wust yur fust.*

**FUZZ**     *Er lives at Ill Fuzz.* This is a proper noun and does not refer to a bastard Italian but to an eminence of the Southern Lenches. Fozzy is also a proper noun but is not the name of a place and does not belong to this section.

**DUST, etc**     *Wur dust thee think thee bist gooin? Thee dussunt ask fer any more a thissun, dust? Dust know what I myuns?*

**NUSS**     *When I wuz in thospital thur wuz a nuss with yaller air. Thee dussunt wan a-known any more about er, dust?*

**PUSS**     There is nothing feline about it and the vowel sound is the same as it is in the others. *Wur dust think er put er puss? Er picked up is change and put it in er puss.*

| **VUSS** | Little used now but common when churchgoing was. *Dust thee know the farth vuss of 'God Save the Queen'? Well, dust?* |
|---|---|
| **WUSS** | *Fust thee wust a-cussin about that nuss and now thee bist a-gettin wuss.* |

Yet Perce is always Perce and a hearse is a hurse. Thirst, more surprisingly for it has the *t*, is always thirst. And it's gettin thundery *agyun*. But when all is said and done and the use of the *u* sound in the Evesham language reconciled as far as may be with the Queen's English in its many forms, the memory remains fresh with the man in the Trade: *Thee shudst a-yurd um a-cussin!*

# More 'Asum Grammar' (20<sup>th</sup> September 1957)

Cheiromys Madagascariensis, apart from being a sickly and indigestible mouthful, happens to be a quadrumanous animal, of the size of a cat. It lives only in that tropical island from which it derives the weightier part of its name. It is probably a disgusting creature. The only reason why it has been allowed to prowl on to this page is a curious one. This disgusting mammal is all that the Shorter English Dictionary can vouchsafe to those of you who may search its two volumes for the origin of the Evesham man's customary mode of greeting to other Evesham men. *Aye-Aye!*

The Aye-Aye of Madagascar was discovered in 1781, but the *Aye-Aye* of Evesham dates from much earlier than that, as the inquiring reader shall one day be able to read for himself in that learned work, long in preparation, but still unpublished, the 'Asum Grammar.'

Although it cannot yet be demonstrated conclusively by etymology, phonology or analogy, modern research into the Evesham language suggests that the interjection *Aye-Aye* belongs to that period in history when there were more shepherds, swineherds and cowherds in the Vale than there are today.

*Aye-Aye, you! Wur ust thee bin lately?* may be a perfectly ordinary greeting from one Evesham man to another in 1957; but few would associate it with the wide-open spaces to which it correctly belong and which gave it a cause.

*Aye-Aye* is analogous not to the sailor's "Aye-Aye," which never opens but always closes a conversation, but to the sailors' "Ahoy!," which is at once a greeting and a challenge. When a seaman, during the night watches, has occasion to bellow "Boat, ahoy!" into the windy darkness over the side, there are certain correct replies to be given and nothing else will do. "Aye-Aye" happens to be one of the correct replies, and one of the friendliest; though in its special circumstances it is spoken more deliberately than the Evesham manner.

In Evesham, *Aye-Aye* means many things according to the inflection of each component *Aye*. These things are impossible to denote typographically so, in view of the time which must necessarily elapse before volume XII of 'Asum Grammar' (Appendix of Tae Recordings) can be completed in the detail it merits, there is no alternative but to provide written examples of speech never intended to be written.

*Yur thee bist, then*: a few examples of the usage of *Aye-Aye* among the professional and other classes in the town and Vale of Evesham.

> **AYE-AYE.** 2. In this use, the greeting, to which the courteous response is *Aye-Aye*, not "Hello" or "How d'ye go?" The man addressed, should he wish to add something to his responding *Aye-Aye* should add *Ow bist?* Pray note that in both instances the first *Aye* has a falling and the second a rising inflection.

> **AYE-AYE.** 2. In this use, both *Ayes* rise. It expresses astonishment or suspicion and among the really succinct it is a hole, self-sufficient interrogative sentence. It was used in the Smithfield furniture saleroom once long ago when a tableful of ormolu ornaments was knocked down to a dealer for something like 145 guineas.

Another example – *Ust thee sin that wench of is lately, you? Aye-Aye...*

It is plain, is it not?, that *Aye-Aye* is not an urban greeting like the *Ave* of the Romans: it will carry further in wide spaces. Yet how it carried to Madagascar and gave its name to a monkey is very hard to say.

# More 'Asum Grammar' (25<sup>th</sup> October 1957)

*It chunt thine: it's isn. Er said er got urn at wum. Ourn's oldern theirn.*

Readers who have digested the extracts printed here from time to time from the 'Asum Grammar' – that learned work long in preparation, but still unpublished – will appreciate that pronouns are the very devil in this part of the world, especially when they are reflexive or demonstrative.

It is odd how the old third person genitives survive so purely in the Vale of Evesham while elsewhere they decay and disappear. The historical reasons for it are themselves well worth exploring, but they have not been explored yet. However, the usage has been explored, tentatively; and in volume II, p.74 *et seq.*, the following will be found.

### REFLEXIVE PRONOUNS

**Third Person**. Nominative, accusative and dative – singular: *isself* (masculine), *erself* (feminine); plural: *thurselves* (all genders).

**Possessive** – singular: *isn* (masculine), *urn* (feminine); plural: *theirn* (all genders)

Examples: *Eee said eed do it isself. Eee bin un shot isself. Er said erd plaze erself. They a done it Thurselves. If it chunt isn it must be urn. It chunt theirn neither.*

The *n* in *isn*, *urn* and *theirn* is, of course, the contracted form of "own": *is own*, *er own* and *thur own*. And *ourn* signifies our own, first person plural. The Evesham language thus contains three surviving *n* endings in the third person and one in the first person of these pronouns: the Queen's English is the poorer for lacking them. In the first and second persons singular, to be sure, the Evesham language shares *mine* and *thine* with the Queen's English; but the grammatical character of these is quite different; if 'own' is required, it must be added. Evesham does not add it, however. *"That pint thur, you: is it thine or mine?"* Sounds an unlikely enough question. But as *"That pint thur, you: is it thine own or mine own?"* it suddenly becomes preposterous, as much out of place as a butt of malmsey in the bar at the Talbot.

### DEMONSTRATIVE PRONOUNS

**Singular**: *Thissun, thattun*; plural: *thaze, um, they, them*.

It is to be noted especially that the plural form of *thattun* is inclined to be various. There is no rule in the matter and the choice is not really governed by case.

Examples: *Thaze be some good paze I a got yur. Be they? Them be some poor byuns eee a got thur. Be um? Um... they ... them. Of thaze, thee canst take thee pick.*

# More 'Asum Grammar' (22<sup>nd</sup> November 1957)

When the strange gentleman asked her where she was going, the pretty maid of the nursery rhyme was alleged to have replied: "I'm going a-milking, sir." In this statement there reposes a wealth of significance for the student of social and literary history which ought not to be overlooked by the student of language:

"Where are you going to, my pretty maid?"
"I'm going a-milking, sir," she said.

At a first glance, one might be forgiven for putting the origin of the rhyme in the early part of the eighteenth century: it seems to belong, by its very colour, to a pastoral England where the rosy-cheeked, blue-eyed innocence of milk-maids is taken for granted as one of the amenities of the countryside.

Look deeper, my friends. There is no need to consider the gentleman's final, ungallant statement that the pretty maid's face is an insufficient fortune. Considerations of English usage in those first two lines make it plain that the conversation is taking place at a more snobbish period, in the nineteenth century. It might have been otherwise if the gentleman had asked the maid where she was a-going. The all-important clue is in that single letter *a* with the hyphen after it.

The "Oxford Dictionary of Nursery Rhymes" confirms that the modern version of the rhyme was "carefully rewritten" in the nineteenth century from words, recorded in 1790 and heard sung in 1698. Sure enough, the earlier texts do not make the gentleman's speech conspicuously genteel and the maid's conspicuously rustic. The snobbery of the "carefully rewritten" text brands itself typically mid-Victorian.

> *"Wur bist thee a-gooin, my pretty wench?"*
> *"I'm a-gooin a-milkin, sir,"* she said.

Such would it have been in the Vale of Evesham. Such might it be today if there were any milkmaids still at large.

*Ooze this a-cummin? Wur bist thee a-gooin? Thee dussunt know whether thee bist a-cummin or a-gooin, you.* These extracts, as the perceptive reader will have suspected all along, are taken from that learned work, long in preparation but still unpublished, the 'Asum Grammar.' They come from volume IX in the long section (pp.143-264) on "Surviving Archaisms," where the descent of that important little *a* is traced from its origin in the Old English and Late Middle English down to its usage in Middle Evesham.

Some authorities decry that *a*. The "Shorter Oxford Dictionary," for instance, describes it as a worn-down proclitic form of the Old English prepositions *an* or *on*. But it is not quite so worn-down as they think, proclitic though it certainly is and very useful too. In the Queen's English, where it is as good as lost, it is variously classified as a preposition of superposition, motion juxtaposition, situation, direction, series, time, manner, capacity, state, process, or action; as a prefix, also. In Chaucer's day, it was a *y*. One recalls the poor old soul who had the misfortune to be "y-clept Euphrosyne."

But in the Evesham language, which has never before this been subjected to any sort of analysis, it is going to be called by the simple name of particle – and the Oxford Dictionary may keep all its thirteen different kinds of *a* preposition, as befits the custodian of a foreign tongue.

*Gooin a-milkin?* Not on your life, Euphrosyne. *Now theest got thee six hundred words, I be a-gooin out fer some tay. Then I be i-cumen back.*

# More 'Asum Grammar' (17<sup>th</sup> January 1958)

*Yunnit chilly?* It is less a question than a greeting and the response may be almost anything between the succinct *Yunnarf, you!*, which is perhaps the most usual, and an octosyllabic curse. The cause of the greeting's appearance here today is, however, nothing to do with the weather, which is mild – curse it!; but is concerned with the following dialogue, which was heard in Castle-street on Tuesday evening:

> *It chunna bad price, is it?*
> *No, it ent.*

*Ent*, in the 'Asum Grammar' – that learned work, long in preparation, but still unpublished – is an object of opprobrium and one of the expressions chosen to illustrate the manner in which the downward path may be taken unawares.

*It chunt* 'ent': *it's 'yunt.'* Pray do not let the partially genteel persuade you to the contrary. On the bus station in High-street the other day, a young mother reprimanded an impatient child with the declaration, "It ent here," with a really vicious aspirate, and it sounded grotesque.

Either you speak the Evesham language, and say *yunt*, the Cockney language and say "ain't" (which has less power on account of its less restricted usage), or the Queen's English and say all sorts of things, such as "am not," "is not" and "are not" in the verb "to be," and "have not" and "has not" in the verb "to have" – though it always depends, of course, on the exact idea you wish to express.

Let us refer to the Shorter Oxford English Dictionary, that strong-box of the Queen's English, which is as good a place as any from which to proceed to more significant matters. You will not find *yunt* in either of its heavy volumes – and small wonder, too: let them stick to their lasts! – but you will find "ain't," which is the orthoepic parent of the illegitimate "ent."

"Ain't" is dated 1778, a very young bird, and is certified to be a later variant of "an't," described as "now illiterate or dialect." "An't" is the descendant of *yunt* – though more versatile, being active in two conjunctions instead of one; and more glib, having been brought up in London Town. The Oxford Dictionary dates "an't" 1706 and describes it as a contraction of "are n't"; a colloquial form of "am not"; and an illiterate or dialect form of "is not," "have not" or "has not."

My friends, there is such a great deal more than this to be said. As you know, English as she is written is but the writable remains of English as she was spoken when the habit of writing began to take root in the people. If you consider the poetry of language, you must surely conclude that *yunt* has no peer. But it has a very sure ancestry.

The Oxford lexicographers would have you believe that the modern "I am not" was formerly "I an't." Say it quickly, without trying to read the apostrophe:

say it humanly, as people really speak and spoke: say it feelingly, as it should be said: and what do you say? *I yunt.* Thus it is proved, over and over again, that the Evesham language (which the pundits insult with nasty words like 'illiterate' or 'dialect') precedes the written English; and is often superior to it.

There is a fair orthoepic test. *Yunt* should occur where the preceding pronoun ends in *i* or *e*, vowel sounds normally pronounced with a *y* 'hook' at the end which affects the succeeding vowel. You can't say "You yunt." It is either *I yunt, Ee yunt, We yunt* or *They yunt*; whereas anything or anybody "ain't" or "an't." As for myself, *I yunt gunner githa any mower this wik. I an't got the time.*

*The old Booth Hall Evesham*

# More 'Asum Grammar' (21<sup>st</sup> February 1958)

1. *Byunn-I?*
2. *Byunnst?*
3. *Byunnee?* (or *Byunner?*)

1. *Byunnus?*
2. *Byuncha?*
3. *Byunnum?*

Here is conjugated, for the contemplation of those people who are accustomed to travel regularly between the Vale of Evesham and the Cotswolds, the interrogative and negative form of the present indicative belonging to the hill dwellers' verb "to be." It will immediately be seen that the principal point of difference between the Evesham and Cotswold language is that the latter is freer with its use of the *b*.

According to the 'Asum Grammar,' that learned work long in preparation but still unpublished, the hill dweller's insistence on keeping his *b* undefiled while the man of the Vale has progressively placed more and more emphasis on the *y* is an interesting subject worthy of more research than has ever been spent on it.

The hill country and the Vale country are ordinarily distinguishable in three ways, apart from considerations of physical geography: the hills have stone buildings, the Vale brick or timber; the hill land is predominantly pastoral or, at any rate, agricultural, and the Vale is all one big garden; the hilly air is energising, the Vale air enervating. Not so readily noticed is that in Cyamdin they say *Byunnum?* and in Braffertn *Yunnum?*, though the two places are practically in sight of each other. There is probably a reason for this, though it is difficult to postulate one with any degree of conviction.

The compiler of the 'Asum Grammar' at present thinks the Anglo-Saxon population of Evesham and the Vale may have been continually increased by settlement from the hills, and that the downhill path has been trodden by hundreds of families down the centuries, bringing their language with them but dropping their *b*s on the way, somewhere near the Seagrave Arms.

> Examples: *Now I be a-tryin ta make thee laugh, byunn-I? Thee bissunt takin it all in, though, byunst? Eee byunt cummin, byunnee? We be, though, byunnus? You be all a-cummin, byuncha? They be a-growin byuns up thur, byunnum?*

# More 'Asum Grammar' (28<sup>th</sup> March 1958)

*Thee plaze theesalf then, you!* said the man in the barber's the other day. He was getting on in years, and none too steady on his feet, but his reflexive pronouns were sounder than most and he was clearly still a force to be reckoned with. In the changing Vale, the reflexive pronouns are tending to be contorted, gradually, by the BBC and other outside influences. Fortunately, in that learned work long in preparation, but still unpublished, the 'Asum Grammar,' they are set forth in all their pristine regularity.

**First Person**     singular: *mesalf, missalf*; plural: *owersalf, owersalves, ersalf, ersalves.*

**Second Person**     singular: *thissalf, theesalf*; plural: *yussalf, yussalves* (but rarely used).

**Third Person**     singular: *issalf* (masculine), *ersalf* (feminine); plural: *thursalf, thursalves* (masculine and feminine)

There is no regular neuter pronoun in the Evesham language, such as can be found in the Queen's English and its many vulgar dialects. Except in certain irregular instances, everything is a *im* or a *er* (and the discerning student will also observe that the indefinite article has only one form, which makes it almost incomprehensible to foreigners). Examples:

*I sez ta missalf, 'Wobby I a dooin yur ut this time a night?'*

*Un ur sez, 'Set thissalf down agyun un po-wur theesalf another drinker two. I a made this mesalf, you. We wunt keep nun a this fer they: we'll a tha lot ersalves, shollus?'*

*Woddus think ee a dunna that clock, you?*

*Ee wuz bust but ee a made im goo agyun.*

*Ee done im isself.*

*Er told im ee could shoot isself fer all er cyurd.*

*If er yunt mower cyurfle url be a dooin erself in.*

Other examples, of similar usages, will readily suggest themselves to the curious, and the 'Asum Grammar' contains no less than 943 specimens, some of which cannot be reproduced here, in the present state of the law. For the time being, there is space left only for two titbits from the glossarial index (vol X):

**OCKUD** – at variance to requirements.

**BACKUDS** – opp. to *forrud.*

# More 'Asum Grammar' (2<sup>nd</sup> May 1958)

"As a general rule," according to a deeply and long-established creator of school English grammars, "a preposition should not be placed at the end of a sentence. It is not strong enough to stand in a place of so much emphasis and importance." It is one of those rules of thumb that ought long ago to have been done away with, given up, packed in and stamped on. It was probably invented by a Victorian maiden aunt in the first place; but it has never done a ha-porth of good and, in these liberal days, it really ought to be dispensed with.

In the Vale of Evesham, nobody ever took much notice of the rule, as one discovers from a quick look into that learned work long in preparation but still unpublished, the 'Asum Grammar.' The section devoted to Prepositions (vol. II, pp.35-241) makes it plain at the outset that, far from being "not strong enough to stand in a place of so much emphasis and importance," the preposition is frequently suited ideally to that final vantage point of expression. Moreover, its strength can be astonishing. Sometimes, it is positively brutal.

In the list of examples which follows, the use of prepositions in the Vale of Evesham at the present time is generally looked over but not very deeply looked into, and the reason will appear. Not all, of course, are sentences using prepositions to end up with. Some uses that fall into this controversial category are, unfortunately, somewhat too strong to bear reproduction in print, what with the present state of the public taste and the criminal law and one thing or another (you too, gentle reader) ever tolerated Bowdlerisation quietly: hence this prefatorial caution. *Yur thee bist, then.*

*Warm agyun, yunnit? Bist thee gunner take thee cwut utha?* Here, to begin, is a very minute preposition – *u.* But it grows. *Er said ers a-gunner bring ern uvver.* Now it is *uv,* which is not to be confused with *of.* Now it shrinks again: *they be a-cummin a-me.* For an interesting reason (which is explored in that section of the 'Asum Grammar' headed Contracted Forms) there seems hardly ever to be a consonantal *w* in the Evesham language.

*They cum tim un teld im.* The preposition, here, is that solitary *t* prefixed to *im.* But what, the reader may well ask, did they tell him? *They teld im to goo arf.* Or words to that effect, but stronger. *"I said to thaze lads, Yur I be un yur I stops,"* P.C. O'Flannel told the magistrates, *"but they replied: Thee get arf up wum or we'll knock thee yud arf."*

*Woddus think on it, you? It's a funny lot on it, yunnit?* This extract from a political discussion in the bar of a small beer-house illustrates an Evesham use of *on* which does not accord with the common modern usage of the Queen's English *on.* It means "about." *I ant sin much onnum lately, you.* This is not the statement of a plum grower concerning the blossom on his trees but that of a country parson concerning the absent portion of his flock. The reader who in unfamiliar with the ways of the Vale must realise also that this *on* is not translatable as a simple "of": it means "more."

There is a similar possibility of confusion in the case of *agyun*, which does not only mean "again." *They a put them paze up agyun the river agyun this year, ant they?* Likewise in the case of *be*, which has nothing to do with *sum*. *I be a-lookin frim be mesalf.* When in doubt *I guz be the book.*

# More 'Asum Grammar' (30<sup>th</sup> May 1958)

Why is it that some people write with their left hands while the majority use their right is a subject for entertaining discussion by those who claim to know the answers. Here, we merely ask the question – why is there a variety of terms used to describe the left-handed? In a part of Yorkshire where these things were investigated long ago, they are called "gawky"; but that term has other uses elsewhere. In the Vale of Evesham, according to that learned work, long in preparation, but still unpublished, the 'Asum Grammar,' there are two words principally used to denote left-handedness – *wacky* and *kaggy*.

Those who are *wacky* or *kaggy* are universally thought to be *ockud* in some way; and here is the only clue to the historical origin of these terms. They cannot refer solely to hand-writing, for the pen is ambidextrous. They belong to the age of craftsmanship.

# More 'Asum Grammar' (27<sup>th</sup> June 1958)

*Exim wur ta goo*, which is the plea of one lost traveller to another, can be readily understood and promptly acted upon, provided the second man comes from the Vale of Evesham also. *Ex* is an extraordinary word, the kind of word which points to the proof of an idea; rather, to the very heart of that idea. But it is not a heart that is easily captured.

According to that learned work, long in preparation but still unpublished, the 'Asum Grammar,' the verb *to ex* is an interesting survival from the sixteenth century; not, as the condescending foreigner might suppose, a pig-headedly contorted version of the established form.

Let us consider what the Shorter Oxford English Dictionary has to say about the established form. The word "ask," it tells us, originated from the Common Teutonic stock which provided Old English, sometimes known as Anglo-Saxon, with the alternative verbs of *ascian* and *acsian*. "Till about 1600," says the S.O.E.D., "*ax* was, but *ask* is now, the literary form." Not a pleasant way of putting it but there is, among the illustrations, the simple and felicitous "I axe no more," dated 1570 – a flower indeed.

Now it is a strange thing, which has not been the subject of comment here before, that the long vowel *a* which the London language employs and the short vowel *a* which is the less pleasant substitute for it of Northerners and Midlanders, are equally absent from the traditional language of the Vale of Evesham. It is difficult to demonstrate these things in cold print without a system of phonological notation such as would unduly tax the gentle reader's patience as well as the gentle printer's resources. Each is already taxed enough. But consider alternatively the Londoner's long *a* in master, fast, last, rasp or father; then the Northerner's and the Midlander's short *a*.

The Evesham long *a*, which is a Western sound, is very near the Anglo-Saxon long *æ*, as in Sumorsæte, the men of Somerset. Why then, should the traveller say *Exim wur ta goo*? Why not simply "ask" him? Now here is purity. *Ascian* or *acsian* was the Anglo-Saxon verb, and the initial vowel *a* was short, not long. It could never be "ask." It was bound to be *ax* or *ex*. And it is *ex*. *Ex* anybody in Asum...

# More 'Asum Grammar' (25th July 1958)

Sally was obviously very sweet; and the fact that she lived in the same alley in her admirer did not in any way dim her splendour in his eyes: she was the *darling* of his heart. She was fortunate, too, in having a poet for her suitor. "Darling of my heart" is not only a term of the greatest affection: it happens to be a very exact use of words.

It is a strange word... *darling*. The song writer's delight, the stage boss's name for his secretary, every mother's whisper to her infant: a common word in everyday use. But oh! so ancient; and, in the English-speaking world, so general and so indispensable. In the 'Asum Grammar,' that learned work still in preparation but still unpublished, the word is dealt with only briefly: it is mentioned, among other *–ling* endings, in the Appendix of Suffixes (vol X, pp.320-392); and the reason for this unexpected brevity is the paucity of popular examples in modern Vale of Evesham usage.

To be sure, the word *darling* is used as a term of endearment in the Vale of Evesham as frequently as it is used anywhere else in the English-speaking world, even if the final *g* sound is entirely omitted so as to make it accord with *spettin, settin, pinchin, yuttin* and *drinkin* – which do not belong to the same part of speech at all, of course.

*Darling* really ought to have its proper *–ing* sound and it is to be hoped that this small contribution to the Vocabulary of Love in the Vale will have gone at least some of the way towards achieving the desired effect. "Darlin" sounds ridiculous. It also sounds Irish.

There are few words that belong categorically with *darling*, as a substantive with the *–ling* suffix; and, oddly enough, those that do are all terms of contempt. It is easy, at a first etymological glance, to make a serious mistake about darling. "Little dear," the unwary student might postulate – an affectionate diminutive, he tells himself, like the *–ette* of modern French, the – *etta*, *-ino*, etc., of Italian. Or, to find simpler analogies at home, in Modern English: duckling, gosling, codling. Now it is true that these farmyard words, ducking, gosling and codling, have the *–ling* suffix for a purely diminutive purpose which is plain for all to see. These examples are several centuries old but there are modern additions to the group and nearly each one – lordling, for instance – is a contemptuous personal designation. The *–ling* suffix can form adverbs from adjectives, nouns from verbs and nouns from adjectives. But it is *darling* we are concerned with here. And *darling* has an ancient, undefiled lineage.

*Déorling*, from the Anglo-Saxon, derives from the déor, dear and the *–ling* suffix. As a noun, in the Shorter Oxford English Dictionary, it means "the object of a person's love; a favourite; a pet." As an adjective, it means "dearly beloved; best loved; favourite." Here, the adjective is prior to the noun; and the *–ling* suffix adds the sense, "a person or thing that has the quality denoted by the adjective." There is only one word comparable in popularity to *darling* and that is sweetheart, which is sometimes rendered in Badsey as *sway-tart*. But, anywhere else, it is a poor second in poetry and etymology. It is a mere Elizabethan (1576) survival, against a more honest, less fancy, Anglo-Saxon beauty – *darling*.

High Street
Evesham

# More 'Asum Grammar' (12<sup>th</sup> September 1958)

"I," said the Sporra, "with my bow and arra. I killed Cock Robin."

The curious may also wonder who killed the Evesham *sporra's* terminal long *o*. Or the Inkbra *sporra's*, for the matter of that. But the truth is that they never had a long *o* between them, terminal or anywhere else.

The 'Asum Grammar,' that learned work, long in preparation but still unpublished, deals at considerable length with terminal vowels; and makes it plain that not euphony alone but pure, honest-to-goodness etymology used on conservative principles, governs the English man in his preference for the *a* over the *o* and vice versa. First, a few simple examples:

> *Wobbist thee a dooin u that yalla borra?* In the Queen's English – What are you doing with that yellow wheelbarrow?
>
> *Eeza ploughin a shalla furra.* He is ploughing a shallow furrow: though not, of course, with the yellow wheelbarrow.
>
> *Wurbis thee a gooin tamorra?* Where are you going tomorrow?
>
> *Eeza gooin ta ketch minniz in the brook, wur it's shalla.*
>
> *Yalla, borra, shalla, furra, tamorra, Inkbra*

…all time-honoured usages, clearly conforming to a rule. It is a rule which has never been publicly stated and laid down until now: but here, Patient Reader, is the eventful moment in which you shall your full money's-worth.

Consider again the little Cock *Sporra* who killed Cock Robin and whom it is customary to called Sparrow. Inquiry reveals that 'Sparrow' has been known since 1668; but the bird is plainly older than that. *Sporra*, on the other hand, traces his name from the Anglo-Saxon *Spearwa* – in which descent he has hardly undergone any change at all and in turn the Anglo-Saxons got him from the Gothic *sparwa* and the Middle High German *sparwe*.

There is not a terminal long *o* to be seen, or heard, you see: the little Cock *Sporra*, like the rest of them and most of us in the Vale of Evesham who call him by his proper name, is even more of a pig-headed Saxon than he suspects.

# More 'Asum Grammar' (17<sup>th</sup> October 1958)

*Wurthellsthabin?* On paper, it looks like a transliterated Tamil curse. On the telephone the other day, it sounded like the complaint of an Evesham man. And it was. Anybody who can express a complaint as succinctly, as powerfully and as poetically as this, deserves the satisfaction he is asking for. So he got it. Thus it was that a small but interesting chrysanthemum show, which had been all but missed, got every one of its just deserts.

Let the superior people who cockily allege the great language that is ours to be merely a "dialect," or even "only an accent," consider this poetical complaint, *wurthellsthabin*, with all of their alertness. For it is one of those things, small in themselves like the chrysanthemum show, which prove enormous truths and confound the unwary.

Shall we waste time for their benefit, then, by attempting a translation? "Where the hell hast thou been?" It sounds like a profane Quaker (and everybody knows there is no such creature) or like the opening taunt of Lucifer unlocking the Gates of Hell: but the line does not appear in the "Inferno;" nor does Milton know it. It is sheer Evesham.

It is a strange thing, for which there must surely be an explanation of some sort, that the Evesham language is richer in references to the abode of the damned than to that of the just.

That learned work, long in preparation but still unpublished, the 'Asum Grammar,' makes no bones of the fact, the curious fact, and devotes an exhaustive section to it in volume IX (The Hereafter), *iger tell*, that Evesham usage which leaves so much understood, has already been briefly examined in an extract published on this page: it is a popular exclamation, rather than an oath, and it has a tremendous weight of history behind it. Geographically, it is commoner in Littleton than in Cropthorne. But the reasons for this will have to be explored another day: we are approaching the bottom of the page, thank God.

One of the enormous truths which is proved by the survival unsullied of *wurthellsthabin* may be indicated by an examination of two simple facts. The first is that it is a unity of speech, quite indivisible, quite unalterable. The second is that its use is common (little children learn it at a very early age; the mature cannot dispense with it; old men and women say very little else) and, most significant, its comprehensible use is utterly independent of accent.

To sum up then, *wurthellsthabin* is not a local abuse of the Queen's English but is quite foreign to that tongue. "Where the hell hast thou been?" sounds like nothing on earth and is so meaningless as to be ineffective. It belongs only to the Vale of Evesham, with such things as *iger tell* and *wot thellbist dooin?*

# Poems & others

Betsy Prig was the by-line on a number of articles which appeared in the *Evesham Standard* in the 1940s and 1950s. She re-appeared, albeit only once, in the pages of the *Journal*. The letters pages of the *Evesham Journal* occasionally hosted poems in Asum from Ron Boulter (who typically signed himself as 'R.G.B.') and others.

## Betsy Prig – She's back again: Alive and Kicking (5th January 1962)

Thee knowst oo it is, dussunt? I fancy a good many onnum thought as I wuz jud, mine tha. But, as I told old Jack, the mon as comes round ta rade the meter now un agyun, I yunt arf as jud as some onnum thinks, mine tha. And if them lot in Swan Lane a got thur yuds screwed on right, they'll sun let all Asum know as I'm alive, *and* kickin.

Aye, kickin! That I be! Mine tha, a this weather as we bin avin, thee assunt arf gotta be cyurful wur thee bist dooin thee kickin. It yunt much good a tryin ta kick too igh in Bridge Street just at the present, I can tell tha. The paths be s'icy this week theest got a bit of a job on ta keep on thee fit all, you.

Still, it chunt no good a-moitherin our pore old yuds about the weather, is it? That's what I told old Jack, anyow. An' ee said: "Aye, that's right, missis. I shud goo on the buz if I wust thee!"

"Goo on the buz?," I says, "Wot thell dust myun, mon? If I guz on the buz, dust thee know ow much they charges ta come up the town from Benjud? I'd a sunner wark, you. Iger tell if I udn't."

"Theest gotta remember another thing," I telled im, "I'm youngern thee."

"Get arf!," ee sez. "Thee bist th oldest old ummun as ever lived anywur round Asum, now bissunt? My old granny used ta rade about thee and they gooins-on afore the Fust War, and er a bin jud fer forty yur or mower, I knows."

"Aye," I said, "I knowed thy old granny. Er used ta rade the "Standard" yurs agoo." It's funny, yunnit, when you comes to ta think onnit... but yur I be, alive... *and kickin!*

# In the Post (20<sup>th</sup> December 1969)

Sur –

The G.P.O., thee mitst recall,
A' got a poster on the wall,
Ta try an' make th' stamp trade better,
"Sumbuddy summer wants a letter."

An' atter yurrin' my tale you,
Thee't maybe think it's very troo.
Abowt a wik frum Crissmus Day,
Th' pussmen getsa 'ollyday,
An' stewdents takes th' letters round,
Thee'st sin 'em trapesin' throo th' town.

I yurs a nok an', waddusno
A gyurl astood thur, in th' snow.
"I gotta pakit yur a thine,"
"'E's rejisturd, thee'st gotta sine."

'Opeful, I gets me pensul out,
Wile 'er guz rummigin' abowt;
Staks 'er letters on a stun,
Shuks 'er bag out upsidown,
An' sez, atter a frown or two,
"It seems I a' furgot 'im you.

We gotsa much, it yun aff grim,
I 'opes as I ant posted 'im."
I thawt, jujin by th' past,
It wunt make much odds if thee ast!

If thee'st a' sin ur face, I dowt
Thee uttn't 'alf a fell abowt.
I didn't cuss ta make 'er blench,
'Er was a jolly-lookin wench.
The kinda sort as makes a chap
Regret th' jenerashun gap.

So if sum reeder sis 'im, see,
Afore I rites ta my M.P.
An' gets this pore wench in a mess,
Plase send 'im on ta this address!
(I nose it chunt wuth much).

R.G.B.

# In the Post (30<sup>th</sup> December 1969)

Sir

That wuznalf a bit o good about that ther pussmuns ollidy in thy paper last wik. Must a set be the jerkum borrel ell uv a lung wile to a thought that un up. Wot with these yer pollytishuns fillin the papers up uv a lot o whats found in the farmyard, an avin nuts uvout oles in thay sez is wuth ten bob in yer penshun, its a change ta see sum sense fer once in thee payper. Exed ol Tom wot sart a Crismus ee ad, an ee sed since is fit ad bin a bit better fer that bit o badger fat ee rubbed on um, eed bin ebble tomble down ta the pub, but wot they sold as beer thosses eed looked atter un is tyme, was allus glad ta get rid uv at the Markit Place. Wen ee tuk the taters t' Asum evry day ee sez is two tith a started playin im up now but ees allus fitherin an cutherin about summut. Ee wuz on about the yung uns uv is daughers, an sez they wuz bwoy and gyurl twins wen thay wuz barn, but now thay be 16 thay be both wenches a luckin at em, sez if all the bwoys in Asum ad ther ayer cut, all the barbers ud be jud in a wik frum overwork, an therd be a yup uv ayer frum the Cross Kayes ta the Regal.

Yours etc.

D.G.C.


# Guzgogs down! (11<sup>th</sup> August 1970)

Sur, -

Thee know'st, no matter 'ow we cuss,
Ol' Ted 'Eath mus' be plased uv us;
The only hindustry in town,
As keeps on puttin prices down!
Guzgogs, be only 'alf th' price
Three yurs agoo, that makes it nice,
An' now as plums a' follad soot,
You feels a pride in grown' froot.
This cosalivin indeks you,
Ull surely drop a point or two,
An' that in spite uv all th' shocks,
From tak a rottin' in th' docks.
Cos' mussin jenly they alleje,
'E guz up cos a froot an' veg!
Whats more thee cossn't odds th' faks
We shawnt be payin sa much taks!

Yours with a patryotik jeschure.

R.G.B.

# Decimal time (27<sup>th</sup> July 1972)

Sir, -

I bin a thinkin' you and all,
Sence everythin' went dessymal,
An' all th' tak bekum so chup,
Now we got yussy reknin up
An, as I've lately yurd it stated,
We'm all sunto be metrikated;
It struck me as it might be prime
If they cud rearranje "the time."

Jus' think we'd 'ave a ten-our day,
Each uv a 'undud minnits say,
Every minnit ud be rekund,
So 'e ud last a 'undud sekunds.
New minnits, min tha, like th' penny,
The old uns ud run out ta many.

Corse Milly Minnit, Dessy Day,
Ud be th' proper thing ta say.
If we all worked in eight-our stages,
Uvout expectin' extra wages,
Th' bennyfits ud be immense,
Tho' ennyboddy with sum sense
Ud see sum things wunt be sa gud,
In th' transishun peeyrud.

Fur instance, clocks and watches wottl
No longer be a lotta bottle –
But while they fixed up summat new,
Dussn't think sundiles mite do?

Then perhaps, they cud arrange
To 'ave th' soler sistum change,
So gooin' round the curran bun,
One 'undud days 'ud be th' run.
'Stead a' wun buthday, as afore,
Theest very nigh be gettin fower.

If they cud make th' penshuns 'igher,
At 20-odd thee cud'st retire.
Th' rest of life ud be enjoyment,
Thur uddn't be no unemployment!

We knows up in Westminster you,
They'm moithered on a thing or two,
But if they was to think a bit,
I reckons they cud tackle it.

Yours cronikolojically,
R.G.B.

# PHGS under the late Doctor Haselhurt (26<sup>th</sup> November 1973)[‡]

Sir

I bin an' read thase letter you,
Sum very eryewdite uns too,
About the 'ighly sykic shock
Fred Archer suffered with 'The Doc.'

I nos I gen 'im cause ta rave
(An! I sin 'im roust 'Jem' Cave).
Atter I bin left a yur,
I cleared th' edge, or very near,
When 'e chanced on sum wench an' me
While crusin' in 'is Model 'T.'

Still, you wasn't allus caught,
Or rarely got more than awt,
An' if thur was cause ta complain,
'is tung was keener than 'is cane.

Tho 'e gen yur 'and a warm,
I can't say as it dun much 'arm,
A fyow more round now, like 'im 'ud
Maybe do a bit a' gud!

R.G.B.

---

[‡] Inspired by a letter to the *Journal* from the author Fred Archer, who had rather particular memories of the late Doctor Haselhurt, former headmaster of Prince Henry's Grammar School. SBB

# Nightingales, a pome (18<sup>th</sup> January 1980)

Sir –

Someone's bin countin' our nightingales,
What a lovely job 'e took!
Ter sit up all night in the soft moonlight
An' make notes in 'is little book!

Someone's bin stayin' awake at night,
Such devotion warms me heart.
An' 'e must 'ave an ear for music too
Ter tell their sweet songs apart!

'E 'ears them in coppice and woodland too,
An' there, 'e can sometimes see
Them rise from their nests, in the nettle-beds,
As 'e sits with 'is back ter a tree!

'E reckons these be ten thousand of 'em,
So 'e's better at countin' than me,
'E sez it's worthwhile stayin' awake,
Ter 'ear their wild symphony!

Margaret Jameson (Tredington)


# Pickers

Dere Sur –

I 'ant rote fur a wik ur two,
'Cos we bin rather moythurd you,
An' I 'ant got the slightest dowt,
Thee knows't wot I be on about.

An' guta'ell you fur a time,
Thee'st rekun growin' 'em a crime,
Nuthin' speshul in the munny,
But all that blahtin' you, was funny.

Sum ses, "The merchants be ta' blame,"
Ur else, "that ruddy wotsisname;
Thase yur thavin' cannin' yids
Uv all thur takin' over bids."

Still – no matter wotum did,
We 'ad ta lave a fyow fur sid!
Them as cum ta pick 'em you,
My blinkin' ykers fur a crew
Sum as cud a' picked, an uddn't.

Them as wanted to, an cuddn't.
But thinkin' as I needed mower,
Picked sum a' th' bloke's next door!

An' you, I an' 'alf got sum mullock,
Scrobblin' thru' that was no frolic,
An' that un in the miny skyurt,
I thinks 'ur found them 'ettles 'eart.
It wasn't 'alf a cyarry on.

But still you lurns as you gus on,
At layst that's ow I've yurd it stated,
(I 'opes I'll sun a gradjewated!)
Like the trees – broke mussly.

Yours

R.G.B.


# Le curé d'où? (31st March 1980)[§]

Sir –

In good old Asum's golden days,
Before the French Connection,
We knew a bit about 'allees,'
It seems on recollection.
We dug between the rows of trees
With all our might and main, Sir,
To finish up, down on our knees,
For just ten bob a chain, Sir.

That Asum's always to the fore,
Goes without hesitation.

---

[§] Inspired by the (as it turned out highly controversial) debate on whether or not to re-name 'The Alley' (the short passage between the top of Bridge Street and the end of High Street) to commemorate the twinning of Evesham with Dreux in France. After lengthy discussions, the Town Council voted 9 to 8 to defeat a proposition that the Council adhere to its original decision not to rename the alley. Or, put more simply, the name got changed. SBB

We worked in tenths in days of yore,
Ere days of metrication.
We dug the plum alleys by chains
On tea and bread and dripping,
But 'graisse à frire' is not the same,
Maybe that's why we're slipping!

Through Dreux Allée we stroll with pride,
Engendered by possession
Of plaques adorning every side,
To aid 'touriste' progression.
So out into the Market Square
With every prospect 'joli,'
To turn and see it standing there,
Our pride and joy, 'La Folie'!

R.G.B.

# The state of Evesham (16<sup>th</sup> October 1980)

Sir –

Hast walked around the town of late
An sin the streets:
Yunt they in a state.

The roads be made of bumps and hollows
The pavements to be broke and going
Except for wur the weeds be growing,
And Abbey Road yunt that a site:

Oi've sin prettier bomb sites,
The railing ther be missing or bust
And them wot yunt, be covered with rust.

Thers posters stuck on empty shops
And kerbing stuns that be all dropped.
They talks about a tourist town,
Yunt it enuf ta make ya frown.

Please, Sir, can we get summutt dun
We know about the spending cuts
But wot about the blooming ruts?
(With apologies to R.G.B.)

F.E. Hampton (Evesham)

'Asum Grammar' contains an assortment of recipes dealing with them and there may be consolation in the possibility that some choice examples may shortly see the light. Gentler readers especially may like to bear in mind, when next in the butchers, that *ships yuds be chup*. Personally, the compiler prefers *pigs fit*.

# More 'Asum Grammar' (6<sup>th</sup> March 1959)

Heaven help the philologist who is landed (and one will be, one day) with the problem of analysing *gissit*. *Gissit* had been thought to have perished about the time of Dunkirk, but it was heard, as fresh as a daisy, in the Market Place at Evesham on Monday; and all praise to its hardiness. But what is it?

Small boy, producing a stamped letter from his pocket: "I forgot about this." Elder boy, dragging the other towards the Post Office: "*Gissit*." He might have put it differently. He might have said, not so many years ago, *Gissit yur*. But there was no need of emphasis, in fact. The small boy knew exactly what he was being told to do, and handed the letter over.

The usage is fascinating because it combines morphological and syntactical interests. It will be found, eventually, in the monumental Linguistic Atlas of England which is at present under construction in the University of Leeds, a work which, kind readers, will have the last say on all these funny little flowers of speech that are purveyed on this page for you every few weeks.

You will not, however, get it for fourpence. In the meantime, therefore, perhaps you may like to know what is said about *gissit* in that learned work, long in preparation but still unpublished, the 'Asum Grammar.' Very well, then: *yur thee bist: yur ee guz agyun.*

*Gissit* is one of the oldest imperatives in the Evesham language. At a first glance, it has a hint of the plural, but this is an illusion. The personal pronoun in the object, which is to be understood and never stated, is always singular: it is always 'me,' never 'us.'

Yet there is no such usage as 'gimmit,' and never was, though it would have been more simply comprehensible. When employed by one person, of course, the first person plural indicates that it is the Pope, the emperor or the editorial writer who is speaking, and the effect is designedly majestic.

With *gissit*, though, the speaker claims no pomp or circumstance. Why, then, does he say it? There is only one simple answer. It is easier. Perhaps it is friendlier, too, if lacking in courtesy. "Give it me" is an entirely formal command, without polite preamble. "Please *gissit*" is impossible because of incongruity. The verb itself is irregular. But the imperative is always *Gissit*.

EVESHAM AND BREDON HILL FROM THE PARKS

# More 'Asum Grammar' (10<sup>th</sup> April 1959)

In their solicitude for youth, the BBC's Network Three, which fulfils the role of prep school to the Third Programme, has this week opened the holiday season with a repetition of the serial, "Starting Spanish." And a very entertaining serial it is, too. Not many language courses have the imagination, or even the daring, to kick off with a bold request such as "Deseamos una habitacion de matrimonio!" Perhaps they have their eyes on newly-weds.

The Evesham language may be said to have a great deal in common with the Spanish and the tempers of the respective peoples are not that dissimilar, either. But what are the prospects, we wonder, for a serial here on "Starting Asum"? There ought to be tons, literally tons, of usable sentences, phrases, usages and ejaculations, all of sound colloquial stock, to be found among the examples in that learned work, long in preparation but still unpublished, the 'Asum Grammar.' *Yur thee bist, then.*

Enoch and Deirdre, who live in a large industrial town in the midlands, are thinking about spending a part of their forthcoming summer holidays cycling and camping in the Vale of Evesham. They know already, from their experience of coach trips on such annual festivals as "Blossom Sunday," that the natives of the Vale speak in a foreign tongue and apparently find it hard to understand what visitors are saying. Therefore, with prudence, Enoch and Deirdre have consulted a teacher of the language who will also be their guide, but not on a bicycle. His name is Chadbury.

**Deirdre**: It won't take us long to get to Evey-shum if it's a fine day, will it Enoch?

**Enoch**: No, especially if we start out early in the morning before the sprout pickers crowd the road.

**Chadbury**: *It chunt no good the tarkin about* Evey-shum, *you. Thur yunt no such place. If thee turnst up in Norton and asks wur* Evey-shum *is, they wunt tell tha. What theest gotta say is Asum.*

**Deirdre**: Oh, what a start, Enoch!

**Chadbury**: *Theest gotta get it in thee yud fust. Now, atter me, both on ya. A-sum.*

**Enoch**: Aye-some.

**Deirdre**: Oi-sam.

**Chadbury**: *No, thee assn't quite got it, mine tha. It's a long 'a,' same uz in plate.*

**Enoch**: Pla-yut?

**Chadbury**: *Plate, thee knowst: what thee yutst arf.*

**Deirdre**: Yutst?

**Chadbury**: *Yutst. Thee bist gettin on lovely, my wench.*

**Enoch**: My wench?

**Chadbury**: Cara mia, ma petite, dilecta mea; *I don't cyur. I was a-tellin tha, afore thee started gettin jealous, that Asum is A-sum. It's a long 'a,' same uz in plate (and don't thee start that* pla-yut *stuff agyun) and it's a very short '-sum,' same as in from when I sez I comes from Asum. Nowst got it?*

**Deirdre**: We'd better get on. We haven't got to Asum yet.

**Chadbury**: *That's my good wench. Theese got it right, now.*

**Enoch**: I don't like this about your good wench.

**Chadbury**: *All right, Enoch. I think theest better stop at Norton for a cuppa tay. Or thee cunst goo wum agyum if thee likes.*

**Enoch**: Wum? What's wum?

**Deirdre**: 'Wum' is what you feel when the sun's shining, silly.

**Chadbury**: *No, it chunt. Wum is wur theest come from. Wum is wur I be a-gooin to. Wur bist thee a-gooin?*

# More 'Asum Grammar' (22<sup>nd</sup> May 1959)

In the ancient seats of learning, there is still time for contemplation before the fight against compulsory Latin enters its critical phase. There is still time to consider the value of the proposed alternatives, German and Russian, and there is still time even to press the claims of other languages, such as Tamil, Swahili, Malayalam, Urdu and Asum, all of which could be important to science in one way or another.

As for Latin, it is a parental language and, no matter who denigrates it or how often, still it will remain – a creation of noble strength and beauty, demanding the deference due to a parent. As for Tamil, Swahili, Malayalam and Urdu, they sound no worse than German or Russian when spoken by natives; and Tamil *looks* extremely picturesque, lending itself admirably to squiggly notices in the public places of the Orient, which is more than can be said of German or Russian.

As for Asum, its merits are self-evident; but, as the Vale happens to be full of visitors this week, those merits ought not to be taken for granted.

> *It chunt sottus it wuz last wik, is it, you?* – *No, that it chunt* (A topical greeting, and its appropriate response).

> *Thee cossunt park thur, thee knowst* – *Waddus myun?* (A topical complaint and its appropriate rebuttal).

These are extracts from a learned work, long in preparation but still unpublished, the 'Asum Grammar,' which sets out to do for the language of the Vale of Evesham what the late Mr. Fowler, in his Dictionary of Modern English Usage, did some 33 years ago for the Mother Tongue: that is, to set down a few signposts, so to speak, by which the man who wishes to speak or write the language without offence may be guided safely on his way. A few simple interpretations then.

| | |
|---|---|
| *Chunt* = It isn't | *Cossunt* = Canst not |
| *Sottus* = As hot as | *Thur* = There |
| *Wuz* = Was | *Knowst* = Knowest |
| *Wik* = Week | *Woddus* = What dost thou |
| *Thee* = Thee | *Myun* = Mean |

There is more in this business, however, than simple interpretation, as long-serving readers already appreciate. Nor is the Evesham language dead. Granted, it has no literary monuments, and is extremely difficult to write, but it is spoken constantly enough, used as a working vehicle of expression, and it is quite scientific.

# More 'Asum Grammar' (19<sup>th</sup> June 1959)

*Ow long yad thissun?* asked the teenage motor cyclist's friend, admiringly, economically and significantly. Admiringly, because the machine was new and good-looking. Economically, because a question that would have required seven words in conventional English has been quite as adequately asked in four. Significantly, because the choice of *yad* instead of *stad* shows that the speech manners of the BBC and Hollywood have penetrated a hitherto invulnerable stronghold of the Evesham language.

Why should the second person singular be buried and forgotten? In the interests of crystal clarity, to say nothing of poetry and a great tradition, there is much to be said in favour of *thou*, *thee* and *thine*. What the teenage motor cyclist's friend should have said, according to the rules categorised in that learned work, long in preparation but still unpublished, the 'Asum Grammar,' was *Ow long stad thissun?* And the strict literal translation into the Queen's English of the term *stad* is "hast thou had."

One would not suggest that the teenage motor cyclist's friend should have actually said "hast thou had," of course. For one thing, the exercise would have produced a very steeplechase of aspiration, with inevitable falls; and, for another, the speaker would have felt and looked a proper Charlie.

Nevertheless, the streamlining of the spoken language to exclude even the 'understood' use of the second person singular is both unnecessary and undesirable; and if, by a remote chance, the teenage motor cyclist's friend should happen to be reading these remarks, let him here and now sit up and take notice. There is nothing 'square' about the second person singular: *thou*, *thee* and *thine* are every bit as efficient as that chromium-plated motor bike, and no less elegant or speedy. If you care for analogy (which is often a simple enough way to prove a point) there is one here.

Consider the question of speed in relation to noise, then agree (before we proceed further) that the ideal motor bike, chromium-plated or otherwise, would make proportionately less noise the faster it went, so that when moving at maximum speed it would hardly produce any sound at all. So it is already with the lamentably neglected second personal singular; and one example alone will suffice to show that there is nothing far-fetched about the argument.

The one example has already been quoted in these extracts from the 'Asum Grammar,' and it is *wurthellsthabin?*, which is pronounced with the emphasis on the final syllable, the preceding three syllables being given equal stress. Now it can hardly be denied that *wurthellsthabin?* is euphonious, efficient, expressive and – above all – rapidly comprehensible. The faster it shoots off the tongue, the less noise it gives off and the more surely does it reach its mark.

The alternative to *wurthellsthabin?* – the only alternative available if the second person singular is to be replaced – is 'wurthellyabin?' Look at it quietly, critically, fairly, calmly, my friends: and then give judgement. Is there one jot or tittle of doubt, in the mind of any reasonable man?

To adopt the style of the lawyers again, is it not proved to the very hilt, de gustibus non disputandum, that 'wurthellyabin?' is utterly untenable in common law, or common euphony, a mere morphological travesty of the facts, unworthy of any place at all in the English language? In the name of Shakespeare, Milton and John Henry Newman, members of the jury, that creeping little 'ya' must be banished from the language.

# More 'Asum Grammar' (14<sup>th</sup> August 1959)

*Itta binna long time, mine tha.* The publishing world, by and large, speaks a more printable language than this; yet this simple remark, made by a contemplative compositor, will be readily comprehensible and acceptable in most of that world, and especially in the remote, quiet corner of it where germinates that learned work, long in preparation but still unpublished, the 'Asum Grammar.'

As a living and somewhat large specimen, *mine tha* will not be easy to handle under the microscope; yet its turn has come, nonetheless, and we must hope that it will not be irreparably damaged in the process.

*Mine tha* is perhaps the most subtle of the Evesham imperatives: it can be an imperative of command, precept or entreaty, according, first, to the volume and tone of voice employed and, second, to the relationship between the person speaking and the person spoken to. For instance, when an Evesham shopkeeper tells his assistant: "Don't forget to lock up the shop, *mine tha!*," he is giving a command, whether the note of exclamation is sounded or not. If he says, *See thee bist yur early tamorra mine tha*, he is probably issuing a precept, on the first occasion or two, at any rate. If he says, *I can't afford ta pay tha any mower, mine tha*, there is probably at least a strong element of entreaty in it.

*Mine tha* is rarely used as a whole, simple sentence, even if it be grammatically a satisfactory one. there are exceptions, though: we have heard a man struggling against the monologue of a bore and using *Mine tha...* as his gambit for getting a word in edgeways. It failed. *Mine tha* has no reasonable translation in the Queen's English; but one feels that it possibly had one many centuries ago. The English verb "to mind," from which this imperative is drawn, has been much weakened by Continental or Latinised interlopers. There are, for example, "Remember!," which is Latin and "Please note!" which is French. *Mine tha* is Old English, in common with so much of the Evesham language; and it is more powerful, direct and musical than its substitutes.

From a practical point of view, it is a pity that the otherwise admirable Times New Roman typeface, in which this is printed, lacks the two Old English characters for *th*. *Mine tha* requires a light *th*, as in 'thin.' Here lies the distinction between the Evesham *tha* and the English 'thou.' The latter requires a heavy *th*, as in 'weather.' *Mine tha*.

# More 'Asum Grammar' (18<sup>th</sup> September 1959)

*Ow bist? Fair to middlin, you...* This conversational snatch, common enough in the Vale of Evesham, demonstrates one of the several meanings of a word which has undergone, and is still undergoing, an interesting development.

*Middlin* (without the final *g* employed in the Queen's English, for in Evesham the final *g* is virtually unknown) was first noticed in 1456, as an adjective of Scots origin, and for its first hundred years or so meant more or less what it said – "intermediate between two things." In 1550 it designated the second of three grades of goods and in 1652 it meant mediocre. But then, quite suddenly, it became an adverb and in 1719 was used, colloquially, instead of "moderately, fairly, tolerably." Colloquialisms all following the same downhill path, it had come to mean, by 1810, "not very well in health."

That learned work, long in preparation but still unpublished, the 'Asum Grammar,' carries the descent of *middlin* considerably further. When an Evesham man (or, more often perhaps, an Evesham woman) speaks of somebody as being *middlin* it is not meant merely that the person concerned is "not very well"; rather, to say somebody is *middlin* is positively to say that he or she is ill, and perhaps very ill.

*Middlin*, in the Evesham language, is a simple substitute for 'ill' or, to be more precise, 'incapacitated by illness.' It carries with it as an adverb of quality the regular degrees of comparison one might expect, but hardly in the form one might expect.

*Middlin* is the positive. Example: *Wur's Jack? – Ee yunna cummin. Ee's middlin.* Interpretation: Jack is absent because he is feeling unwell, slightly ill, or off-colour enough to be incapacitated. But there is no cause for alarm. Jack's all right. He may even be just a pessimist.

*Pretty middlin, you* is the comparative. Example: *Jack ant come agyun today. Ow is ee? – Pretty middlin.* Interpretation: Jack is not so well as he was yesterday. He has probably called the doctor. It is doubtful if we shall see Jack out and about for some time. But, of course, we wish him well.

*Very middlin*, or *middlin* qualified by a different term of greater strength is the superlative. Example: *Jack ant bin for wiks. Ow's poor old Jack? – Very middlin.* Interpretation: Jack is seriously ill.

Now, as every schoolboy knows, an adverb (which *middlin* is) qualifies a verb, an adjective or another adverb. What, then, does *middlin* qualify? The answer is in the verb 'to do.' The question which produces *middlin* in the answer formally asks how Jack does or did.

# More 'Asum Grammar' (30<sup>th</sup> October 1959)

One of the obstacles between spoken speech and its accurate realisation on the printed page is the unfortunate adequacy of the Western alphabet. The ABC is a rough and ready instrument, which was not designed for half the uses it is nowadays called upon to fulfil.

Take, for example, the statement: *Thee dussunt cyur, dust?*, which is common enough in the Vale of Evesham. *Cyur*, by the simple phonetic system employed in the reproduction of these extracts from the 'Asum Grammar' (that learned work long in preparation but still unpublished) looks exotic, as if it might signify a huge, larger-than-life, snarling dog; yet it is in fact the only word among the four quoted that belongs quite regularly to modern Accepted English. There is a remaining gulf between what is sayable and what is writable; and, as far as the general reader is concerned, that gap is absolutely unbridgeable.

*Cyur* is, simply, 'care.' A case could probably be made out for its development from 'care,' through 'cay-yur,' to *cyur*. But there is no need of it. Vowels do get lengthened or shortened, in that fashion; and not only in English, either. There seems to be a point, however, at which development stops. Consider the Accepted English word 'more.' In the Vale of Evesham, from time immemorial, it has been pronounced *mower*, as if it were a machine for trimming lawns. But it is very doubtful if *mower* is going to become 'mwur' in the foreseeable future.

Then there is that lovely word, 'flower.' How shall the Evesham version of that diphthong be accurately recorded with just the ordinary alphabet? It cannot be done. Such brown cows as there may be in this predominantly market-gardening area have no connection whatever with the speech of the people. Is there, then, a readily adaptable phonetic notation? Unfortunately not: typographical limitation preclude it. And so, because the finer points of the consonants and the rich music of the many vowels cannot be set up in printer's type, the present simple scheme – inadequate though it is for *cyur*, *mower* and so much else – will have to stay. *Yur thee bist, then.*

> *If thee bissunt mower cyurfle, theelt a them payurs a thine goo rotten, you. So theetst better take cyur ormum, you, addunst? I sin a fyow, mine tha.*

*Fyow* is perhaps the word that throws out the most formidable resistance to simple phonetic treatment. If you happen to be a resident native of the Vale of

Evesham, you will certainly know *fyow*. For the assistance of readers who may lack that qualification, the only sound to be in any way related to *fyow* is that made by a cat with a common cold, stifling a sneeze.

THE BELL TOWER FROM BENGEWORTH

# That it Yunt! (11th December 1959)

"I was at Offenham the other week," a correspondent writes, "and I asked an old school-mate a question. The reply I got was *Chuntdunnuppit*. I wondered if Ben Judd could tell me what the question and reply was. Both were intelligent."

Ben Judd will try, though he wonders what there can be, even in Offenham, that *chuntdunnuppit*[**]. After all, it is the common belief in Offenham, Littleton, Badsey, Bretforton and all such hubs of horticulture that this is going to be the most *dunnup* winter for many years. Something in Offenham, however, still survives... some mysterious something than *Chuntdunnuppit*. The outlook is not extremely hopeful, though: note the emphasis placed by the old school-mate on *it*. What he may mean, pessimistically, is that is *Chuntdunnuppit buttittullbee...*

---

[**] [Brief note, 18-12-1959] *Chuntdunnuppit* = It is not done up yet. A gloss left out of last week's article.[**]

# Book Review: Two rude Littleton words (25<sup>th</sup> December 1959)

**Ben Judd, *Yur thee bist* (Grist-Bitung, Trincomalee, Rs. 13.50)**

*Yur thee bist agyun,* in fact. Here, for your Christmas bookshelf, is another of those revealing glimpses of life as it is lived of language as it is used, by the not-so-common people of the Vale of Evesham, at work and at play. It consists, for the most part, of essays on subjects taken from the 'Asum Grammar,' that learned work which has been so long in preparation but is yet unpublished. The unassuming title of this volume might lead you to dismiss it in advance as very probably being "the mixture as before." How wrong you would be, though!

As the author explains in the preface (which, being an Anglo-Saxon, he entitled 'Foreword') the purpose of this book is that of entertainment pure and simple; and the entertainment is not only for the benefit of such as know a subordinate adverbial clause of manner when they see one.

In fact, you may feel disposed to ask yourself – after you have passed page 14 – whether this man Judd is putting the pleasures of grammar for its own sake so far behind him that he is in danger of becoming a music hall act. Some of the gags in these pages could never have been printed by a British publisher. Who, one wonders, are Messrs. Grist-Bitung, or Trincomalee?

'*Worst thee a bin a my wench?*' is the title (and first line) of some plaintive verses which will remind the genuine student of dialect that Barnes in his Dorset was a wise man to avoid the subject.

The verses are set to music, too... '*I a sin tha!*' is a composition of the same order; and it has little or nothing to do with the bowl of hyacinths which forms the subject of the illustration at the top of the page.

Other features of this preposterous volume are: an essay on the advantage of having a *Bald Yud*; a dialogue between two *shuppuds a Yubberton*; a short examination paper on 'Yokel History'; and a discourse on the 'Morphology and Semantics of Two Rude Littleton Words.'

What more can you expect for Rs. 13.50?

# Secrets of the Garden

## Ben Judd, *I a Sinner* (Grist-Bitung, Trincomalee, Rs.4.50)

This low-priced little paperback, with its sensational picture on the cover, may not be allowed into Ireland; but why should Vale of Evesham readers worry about that? To them it will prove a boon, enabling them to understand without effort the full meaning of those mysterious words uttered by the sages of Bretforton, Littleton, Bengeworth and such places: *I a sinner*.

It explains the true nature of *sin*, which is more than you are entitled to expect for the money. It recounts, in dialect form (for easy comprehension by those not addicted to analytical study) how one man and one woman, in the joy of their youth, behaved on a certain summer evening, in a certain garden, long ago. The following extract, taken at random, will have mad queues stamping at the bookshop doors:

> *"Wodduss myun?"*
>
> *"Thee assunt gotta a thissun."*
>
> *"Wot thelldust myun? It chunt thine."*
>
> *"I knows. It's isn."*
>
> *"Ee wunt missim."*
>
> *"That ee ull."*
>
> *"Gissim yur! Gissim quick afore ee comes."*
>
> *"That I never sholl. If thee wantst im, theetst better gettim fur theesalf."*
>
> *"Ai, that I ull, then..."*
>
> *"Wobbiss thee up to?"*
>
> *"I'm a gunnav im, you. Thee trouble thee yud uthee own business... Ease mine now."*
>
> *"When thy old mon comes along yur, knowst what eel say, dussunt? Eel say, ''Ast thee sin that wench as pinched that red rose bud?' Then I shall tellim, 'Ai,' I'll tellim, 'Ai, I a sinner'."*

# 'Asum Grammar': The Alphabet (21$^{st}$ October 1960)

**A.**

It is the first letter of the Greek, Hebrew and Latin alphabets; and therefore a thing worthy of your respect, not only for its primacy but for its antiquity. Among caesars and centurions and their pals, it was the shortest and sweetest of the prepositions belong to the ablative. Among market gardeners, sprout pickers and our pals of the present day, it is the briefest yet more comprehensible of interrogatives. It survives, very healthy, not requiring embellishment as time progresses, as many words do. It stands secure, in a very strong position to resist any attempt to shorten it or whittle it down. Here's to **A**, and to the *muck-yup* with "I beg your pardon" and suchlike artificialities!

Readers with powerful memories, very acute analytical faculties, profound insight and good hearing, will probably have guessed by now that the foregoing remarks really belong somewhere else: on the pages of a less ephemeral work than a mere newspaper (for newspapers are not lasting things any more, are they?). As far as the present writer is concerned, the reader – like the customer – is always right, especially if he is a critical reader. Week in and week out, month in and month out, year in and year out, you pay your hard-earned fourpences. And your fourpences, by coalescence so to speak, come to constitute a formidable investment; so that you are entitled to much more than your simple four penn'orth. You shall know what's going on; and what's in the wind.

That learned work, long in preparation but still unpublished, the 'Asum Grammar,' has not been sleeping these past twelve months. The enormous labour has continued: the Old English sources have been searched and researched; the Middle English sources have been explored again; the Vowel Shifts, experimentally charted, have been under the closest attention; and now Christmas is coming round again.

Nevertheless, it is always best to begin at the beginning; and the beginning is **A**. Next week, on this page there will be an announcement of interest to readers who are market-gardeners. And there will also be an examination of the Asum *A*.

# Asum Alphabet: A (28$^{th}$ October 1960)

*Aze what osses yut*, said the awful little boy, by way of reprimanding his slightly deaf companion for not being polite enough to say, "I beg your pardon." *Ay, but it chunt all they yuts*, the deaf one replied, competitively. He was quite correct, of course. And he might have added also that *A* is not only fodder for horses: it is the prince of interrogatives: as a part of speech it is as unique, as simply expressed, as the question mark itself, which is its counterpart in punctuation. *A* has, nevertheless, many different shades of meaning. These are governed by syntax, which has nothing whatever to do (O new reader) with costs in the Divorce Court, but is simply concerned (as old readers understand) with that ancient rule of the best grammarians:

> *It chunt what thee sest; it's the way thee sest it. Yur thee bist, then.*

'Andiamo,' as they say in Rome. Used at the beginning of a sentence, *A* is invariably a mere methodical device whereby one person makes sure the next is fully awake before he starts casting pearls before the swine. For instance: *A, bist thee a-gooin wum now, you?* The correct reply is either *Nottit, you!*, *Aye* or *Woddus myun?* (the latter, if the person addressed has heard the question but has not completely comprehended its significance).

*A* is not usually a familiar form of address; nor is it really polite. It is mostly used for comparative strangers. *A, Fred*, on the other hand, is always a familiar form and it normally gives Fred to understand that what is about to follow will be either a confidence or a request for a favour, such as a small loan until Friday.

> *A, Fred: dust know what that wench said?*
> *A, Fred: come yur a minute, ut?*

At the end of a sentence, *A* is rather like a question-mark underlined, or in italics: it is there for emphasis; and occasionally it has a plaintive quality, like the Latin 'nonne' when uttered by a pessimist.

> *Wurthell dust thee think thee bist a-gooin, A?*
> *Thee assunt binna drinkin my beer, A?*

*A* can also be used ironically (though there is hardly a place for irony in a grammar) and with the preposition *up.*

> *A-up, yurs a wench a red air a-cummin atter thee.*
> *A-up, wurbiss thee a-puttin thy big fit?*
> *A-up, it's time I gottarf up wum agyun.*

Next – *B* (Unless any kind reader has anything further to add about *A*).

# The Asum Alphabet: More about A (25ᵗʰ November 1960)

**A** (continued)

Several students have been good enough to share with us their own experiences of the Asum *A*. I think it was Mr. George Harcourt, of Culham College, who mentioned one little vulgarism which, though familiar to all of us, yet missed its place in the first brief analysis: *Igertay.*

For visitors to the Vale and newcomers to the course, it is probably necessary to explain that this is an interjection (that is, if it is to be treated as a single part of speech, which might be as well) and it means, more of less, "Well, I never!" or "Goodness gracious!" or something equally genteel and inept. It is a shabby genteel substitute for the time-honoured *iger tell*, which is infinitely more expressive, valuable, literary, healthy and moral, my friends, than any of those four-letter words included by the late Mr. Lawrence in that notorious book.

Every priest and every preacher (and I would rashly claim authority for saying so from the Vatican Council and the Convocation of Canterbury, in joint session) ought to be familiar with that part of the 'Asum Grammar' (that learned work, long in preparation but still unpublished) which deals with the philological and theological implications of *iger tell*. If it's orthodoxy you want, we have it.

The 'Asum Grammar' favours *iger tell* in preference to *igertay*, which it nevertheless notices. It also notices another curiosity: *igertannerver*, which is a relic of the old days, quite long ago, when Hanover and all it stood for was an object of execration for the Common People of England.

By the same process of deduction it might possibly be argued that the *A* in *igertay* is Hades without its aspirate or its case ending. It's possible. But *igertannerver* is etymologically clearer and needs no hypotheses at all. It must date from the time of George I (1714-1727) or George II (1727-1760) and it must be at least faintly (and possibly strongly) Jacobite. Why such conviction, gentle readers? Let me explain.

The substitution of Hanover for Hell was done by people who considered that it was an equivalent sort of destination for the accursed: otherwise they might have said *igertevvun*, which they didn't. Hanover meant nothing at all to the English until Fat Queen Anne (who was a Stuart by birth if not regal by right) died in 1714, and the Elector of Hanover ascended the throne as George I in the following year. James Edward Stuart (*de jure* James III, but known to the Establishment as the Old Pretender) tried his luck, in the Fifteen, and failed: the greatest king that England never had, yet much loved by the people. *Igertannerver*: the expression may have its roots in the Fifteen.

Or in the Forty-five? The attempt by the unfortunate Charles Edward, *de jure* Prince of Wales, to restore his father, in 1745, was made against the Elector of Hanover, George II – whose first waking words when roused from sleep with the news of his accession were "Zat is von big lie!"

On his wife's death-bed, she urged him to marry after she was gone and he made what has come down to us as a rather rich remark in reply: "Non, j'aurai des maitresses!"

All they could say in Evesham was *igertannerver!*

# More 'Asum Grammar': Resolution – Let's hear more of… Yunnit! (6<sup>th</sup> January 1961)

The first week of a new year (may all 52 of them be happy, prosperous *and* peaceful for you!) is a time for beginnings and optimism and, now and again, for resolutions. I say "now and again" because resolutions are apt to be somewhat brittle articles, as easy to break as they are to make. Resolutions ought to have a firm purpose of amendment as their heart and core; and that purpose ought to be fixed by a reasonable process: otherwise there is no sense in them.

For example, honest people who have always been in the habit of saying *Yunnit?* when seeking affirmation for a proposition would undoubtedly be very ill-advised to resolve henceforth, at this stage of this Year of Grace, to express themselves differently, by saying "Isn't it?," or some such nonsense, believing it more polite. The plain fact is extremely plain. *It yunt.*

According to 'Asum Grammar,' that learned work which has been long in preparation but is still unpublished (have patience, Loyal Reader!) there is nothing impolite or vulgar about *Yunnit?*, which rhymes with punnet, run it, and Mr. Dunnett.

*Yunnit?* is the simplest, cleanest, pleasantest, most expressive way of saying exactly what has to be said, nothing more and nothing less; it is by far the best tool for the job it has to do. The Queen's English has nothing like it. It fulfils its function with complete efficiency, without having the slightest need of one, single diacritical mark. It commends itself to Dr. Otto Jespersen, with my compliments.

Well, then: do not resolve to do away with *Yunnit?* If you feel inclined to abolish something by way of sacrifice, abolish 'Ennit?,' which is a coarse, back-sliding vulgarism. By way of guarantee that this ancient, respectable and efficient language of ours shall survive inviolate throughout the coming year, why not resolve to use it more? Make it a habit, for example, to say *yunnit, yunnI* and *yunnum, yunnee, yunner* and *yunnus,* pretty often (in the correct context, of course) from now on. Here is the conjugation, in case you need it:

| | |
|---|---|
| *YunnI?* | *Yunnit?* |
| *Yunnst?* | *Yunnus?* |
| *Yunnee?* | *Yuncha?* |
| *Yunner?* | *Yunnum?* |

It is no use complaining, wistfully, that the Common Language is being watered away if it is you who are doing the dilution. Hold your heads up high, therefore, at the dawning of this New Year and continue as you always did, to speak the language of our ancestors. What was good enough for them is good enough for us. *Yunnit?*

# More 'Asum Grammar': Asum Alphabet – B (17th February 1961)

*"No, your worship, er wasn't what you'd call polite: er said I was a silly old B– and B– old fool, and er telled me to B– arf."*

The witness was not invited to complete the missing words. There was no need of it. The magistrates, the advocates, the defendant most of all, knew perfectly well that the first B– was a common noun, the second an adjective of quality and the third an intransitive verb.

It is necessary not to overlook these ciphers when considering the second letter of the Asum alphabet: their use is long established and there is every indication that it is continuing despite discouragement. According to the 'Asum Grammar,' that learned work long in preparation but still unpublished, there is no good reason why words such as these should ever have been so misused; but they have been, they continue to be and they probably always will be: so that's that.

There is probably no remaining reason why the second B– in the courtroom should not be identified. It is 'bloody.' There are some etymological antiquaries who will tell you that the term is a contraction of a medieval oath, 'by Our Lady' but this seems to be rather unlikely.

As for the other two B–'s, which have identical spellings but are different parts of speech, there are books in public libraries which contain them quite unselfconsciously; but they do not usually appear in respectable newspapers, and this for two reasons: first, because they are impolite and, second, because the usage is semasiologically absurd, except in the reports, happily rare, of certain criminal classes. Let us pass on, then:

| | |
|---|---|
| *I be* | *We be* |
| *Thee bist* | *You be* |
| *Ee is* | *They be* |

The present indicative of the Asum verb "to be" is almost as simple as that: and perhaps this is enough to show that the verb is not by any means as irregular and defective as the Queen's English verb "to be."

*Be* originates in the very paternal fountain-head of language, deriving from the Sanskrit stem *bhu-*, from which Latin got the stem *fu-* and Old English its verb béon, to become. The odd thing is that in southern England (which normally includes the Vale of Evesham where the geography of England is concerned) *be* did not come into common use until the first half of the 13ᵗʰ century and it was gone soon after the end of the 16ᵗʰ, except in this verdant Vale and a few other places. Earlier, they had used 'sind' (as in Modern German) and later 'are' became standard.

There is no trace of 'sind' in Modern Asum. Nor is there any trace of 'are.' It may not be improper, therefore, to deduce that the majority of our ancestors were (as so many of their descendants became) quite satisfied with their medieval manners of speaking.

The period between the Battle of Evesham, in 1265, and the incorporation of the Borough, in 1605, holds nearly all the development by which the Asum language became what it is today. From a simply historical point of view, that is what makes the 'dialect' (as some people call it) interesting. *Be* is also a preposition and an adverb.

> *Thur wuz I, a-settin thur all be meself. I sinner, down be the New Bridge.*

Let the perceptive perceive a thing of wonder. With this *be* (spell it how you like) the Asum language has survived the Vowel Shift. As we have agreed before, our ancestors were pig-headed cusses. While all the other English changed their *be* to 'by,' they made no change. For them, a well-tried way was good enough.

# When you think of it: More 'Asum Grammar'

*"Ustad thee money it?"* Between one plum grower and the next, it is a question which is bound to be asked once or twice before the end of the summer, so there is probably something to be said for considering one of it's more profound implications (Printer, kindly leave that apostrophe alone) here and now, while there is still time for contemplation.

According to that learned work, long in preparation but still unpublished, the 'Asum Grammar,' it is one of the authentic signs, by which a true-born native of the Vale of Evesham may be recognised, that a man shall say "it" when a foreigner might say "yet."

> *Er ant bin it*
> *I ant sinnim it*
> *Thee assunt yuttum it*

The meanings are too self-evident, the phrasings too noble, to call for anything by way of translation. Yet, as I say, the form of 'it' demands contemplation. Let us therefore contemplate it.

The consonantal 'y' is not omitted because of bone idleness or ignorance of 'correct' usage but simply because it is an unnecessary obstacle to smooth expression. As a matter of fact, the 'y' is a victim of mutation but as the change happened long ago, before any of the surviving records of the English language were written down, there is nothing to be gained for pursuing it too far. But I mention this matter of antiquity simply to indicate that *it* for 'yet' is quite respectable, having been well known to our rude Anglo-Saxon forefathers whom, pig-headed in our resistance to needless change, we so faithfully resemble. They, moreover, were awkward enough to spell it with a kind of 'g,' if they ever had occasion to write it.

*Yet a-while*, a phrase commonly found in the Evesham language (among others) is also very old; but here the 'y' is always pronounced in the modern fashion, and this for reasons of emphasis: the accent is invariably on the first syllable of the phrase. *I yunna cummin yet a-while, you.* Observe that it is used only in sentences conveying a negative import. It is thus a very exact form and the language possessing it is rich indeed to have such finely sharpened tools. It will be a sad day when *yet a-while* goes.

# More 'Asum Grammar': Accept my apologies (17<sup>th</sup> March 1961)

*Thee cossunt put thine down thur: theest gotta puttim up yur, I tell tha!* The man in charge of the car park at the fête unconsciously demonstrates three facts: first, that he is a native of the Vale of Evesham; secondly, that he is not ashamed of it; and, thirdly, that he knows what he is talking about.

Concomitantly, he demonstrates three more facts: first, that his language is capable of being readily understood by the common people – for the common motorist promptly moves the offending vehicle; secondly, that the second person singular, far from being useless and woolly, is rather apt and exact – for in this instance *thee, cossunt, thine, theest* and *tha* refer unequivocally to one singular person, to wit, one particular motorist; and thirdly, that there was a place among the translators of the New English Bible for this car park attendant – for the translators apparently think the second person singular is out of date but he knows it isn't.

*When thee bist a-tellin the tale about this yur mon uz udn't lave is five yoke of oxen* – he would certainly have told the clerical professors – *theest got uz ee said,* 'Please accept my apologies.' *Thee cossunt put that you, theest better put,* 'I pray thee have me excused.' *Everybody knows that they myuns, donum?*

The foregoing fantasy, combining the sublime with the ridiculous, is meant as a simple illustration and offered diffidently, in support of *thee*. Not so diffident, by half, the 'Asum Grammar,' that learned work so long in preparation but still unpublished, has something to say (in volume IX, pp.392-450 *et seq.*) about the Awful Dilemma of the Translator. It deals primarily, of course, with colloquialisms translated from one popular dialect into another: for example, from the Cockney 'Gawd lav a duck!' into the Cotswold equivalent 'Lor lummy!' But the dilemma is always as awful.

On the one hand, you can render word for word, keeping the word-order as faithful as possible. On the other hand, you can digest the original sense to the best of your ability and make a paraphrase of it. The Bible team obviously proceeded by the second method. Well, it was **their** business. Like the late Monsignor Knox (who did a modern R.C. version a few years ago), they have made a down-to-earth, common denominator job of it, easy to read and understand. The 16th- and 17th-century translators, on both sides of the Channel, used the first method as far as their scholarship allowed and made good the deficiencies in their Greek with the most splendid English ever printed; and they produced sublime works of art, timeless and irresistible. Please accept my apologies…

# More 'Asum Grammar': Health and Happiness (7th April 1961)

Long may they live, in happiness and prosperity, all those young couples who flocked to Four Shires altars at Eastertide and took each other for better or worse; and may it always be for better. The same greeting, also, to all those other young couples who, having exchanged the same vows at other altars, have now flocked to the Four Shires, on honeymoon.

Honeymoon couples are always quite easy to identify: they are at once young, well-dressed, on holiday when other people are working, solicitous, dreamy and above all *inseparable*. On my way to the office on Tuesday, I counted three between Evesham Bridge and the Town Hall, a distance of about three hundred yards. It was raining but they were oblivious to the rain. They probably haven't noticed the rain yet, for the great thing about honeymoon travel is that it is the one kind of travel which produces only pleasant memories.

In any kind of travel, however, it is a useful advantage to understand, at least to some extent, the language of the country. Abroad, it is enough if you can tell the time of day, count your change, get food, drink and a bed, and catch trains. At home it is by no means as easy as that. A southerner going north, for instance, needs to know that to sup is to drink, not to eat supper.

Here, in the Vale of Evesham, the foreign visitor (that is to say, he or she who hails from north of Bidford, south of the Seagrave Arms at Weston Subedge, west of Wyre or anywhere east of the hills) really needs a little book of phrases. As the tourist trade is not sufficiently advanced to provide such a phrase book, and neither public nor private enterprise can do it except at an extravagant cost, there is obviously no alternative but to start its modest work here and now, for nothing, with a few relevant extracts from that learned work, long in preparation but still unpublished, the 'Asum Grammar.' *Yur thee bist, then.*

> **WENCH** and **UMMUN**. The difference is simply stated, as one of age. Most of the Easter bridegrooms married wenches and they are not to be pitied for it, for in this Vale a wench is not what she is in some other parts of England: an Evesham, or a Badsey, or a Littleton *wench* is quite simply a desirable young *ummun*.

The visiting bride, therefore, need feel no dismay if somebody addresses her kindly as: *My wench*. The visiting bridegroom, however, may as well stay around. For *my wench* does not mean 'my girl' in the sense that a business-like Cockney means when he says, 'ma gal'; it is warmer.

> **WORSER**. This is not a double comparative. It is the simple question, "Where is she?"
>
> **WURZEE**. This is the masculine form of the above.

It needs to be noted that in the Vale of Evesham there is only one *she* and that is the pig at the bottom of the garden. All, all other feminine creatures, without exception, are *er*. On second thoughts, perhaps a phrase book is not necessary. It is better to find out these things unaided.

# It's free speech in a free country (5<sup>th</sup> May 1961)

In Ceylon, where the sun shines every day of the year and darkness falls without fail at seven o'clock precisely, there is a fearful row going on between the Simbalese and the Tamils. The former, who are the aboriginal and Buddhist majority, want theirs to be the national language; and the latter, who are mostly Hindus with roots in Mother India, are defending their freedom of speech (and of religion) by a civil disobedience campaign. There will be a sort of civil war in that island paradise. Eventually, however, Old Judd's prediction (issued without charge to readers of this paper) will be fulfilled: the minority will succeed. For you cannot kill a language by Act of Parliament any more than you can kill a religion by Act of Parliament.

*Theest gottim*, the evening paper seller cried the other day when the City gent found he'd caught his paper instead of dropping it into a High Street puddle. The words may have mystified the City gent a little, and amused him a little more, but of bloodthirst there was not a trace in his expression as he moved briskly onward to the station. After all, it's a free country. This kind of freedom, which has been 1,500 years a-growing, is the easiest of all freedoms to take for granted as a matter of fact. But look at its fruits; Chaucer, Shakespeare, Milton, Newman and the paper seller who's a thousand years behind the times with his *theest gottim*.

Why *him* for a not particularly virile evening paper? It's a strange thing, this almost complete lack of a neuter pronoun in the Vale of Evesham. When an object is directly referred to, it is always as *him* or, to be more exact, *im*.

| | |
|---|---|
| *Theest gottim* | *Gissim yur* |
| *I ant sinnim* | *Puttim thur when theest finished uvvim* |

In each case, the *im* can refer to equal clarity and correctness to a newspaper, a spanner, or a bottle of beer. Linguistically, a stranger to the district would not be surprised if some nouns, and their pronouns accordingly, belonged to the feminine gender. But when a Badsey, or a Bretforton, or an Evesham man says… *theest gotter, I ant sinner, gisser yur, putter thur when theest finished uvver*… he is certainly not talking about a newspaper, a spanner or even a bottle of beer. He's talking about a woman. And not very graciously, either.

Likewise with the nominative case. The feminine personal pronoun is invariably *er* in the nominative. The only *she* in the Vale of Evesham, as it is more than once explained in that learned work, long in preparation but still unpublished, the 'Asum Grammar,' is the pig, or rather sow, that lives in the sty at the bottom of the garden.

*She* is a long way in time and space from that tropical island where they are going to start a war for the right to use their own language. Perhaps it is one of the shortcomings of an otherwise successful colonialism that the natives were never taught how menacing language can be if it is not funny.

# More 'Asum Grammar': 'Chunt Ent' (18<sup>th</sup> August 1961)

What is the difference between *ent* and *ant*?

The question came from Shipston. A visitor from that town had been listening to an Evesham conversation, which probably went something like this:

> *Ant er binnit?*
> *No, er* ent *cummin.*

This really was deplorable and one's first reaction was to think that if vulgarism as nasty as this is creeping into the everyday speech of the younger generation then there must be some protest: perhaps one should reconsider one's offer to paint a strike banner for the teachers.

On second thoughts, though, moderation prevails: for heaven's sake pay them their extra few millions (it is a mere drop in the ocean, anyhow) and expect them, in the Vale of Evesham at least, to eradicate this horrible, detestable 'ent.' Everybody knows it should be *yunt*. Everybody knows, without consulting that learned work, long in preparation but still unpublished, the 'Asum Grammar,' that it should be *yunt*.

For the benefit of further visitors to the Vale, however, a short extract may help to make the situation perfectly clear to all.

*Ant er binnit?* It is a euphonious, economic and quite regular way of saying: "Has she not been yet?" or "Hasn't she been yet?" Foreigners should be careful to note that *ant* is pronounced slowly, with a wide open mouth, and not roundly as if we were respectably referring to uncle's wife.

The revolting retort – *No, er* ent *cummin* – shows from what directions our great and ancient language is now being threatened. 'Ent' is a slovenly form of "ain't." It just will not do. It will not do, because there is to be preserved in the Evesham language the distinction (lacking in the Cockney and Birmingham tongues) between the verbs "to be" and "to have" in the negative forms as used in that overheard conversation. It is too short a journey from *ant* to *ent*.

*Ant* is "has not" and *yunt* is "is not" and there should really be no need to point out that the twain ought never to meet if the strength of the language is to be preserved. Certainly, "ain't" can belong to either verb indiscriminately; but that is an historical accident which, however interesting, should not be allowed to render *yunt* superfluous.

*It yunt as if they ant bin telled. Mine tha.*

# More 'Asum Grammar': Thine and Mine (15<sup>th</sup> September 1961)

Let's being this term with a short consideration of two good old-fashioned words, *mine* and *thine*. In the Vale of Evesham we are one of the few surviving communities in England who use both of these words habitually.

According to the 'Asum Grammar,' that learned work long in preparation but still unpublished, *thine* is by far the more interesting specimen, whose passing from common usage would be an unfortunate event. Why? Because it is more useful than its alternatives. It is much less trouble to say, *Chunt mine, it's thine* than to say, "It isn't mine, it's yours." It sounds better, too, being more mellifluous and less tight-lipped; and it is equally courteous.

### Yours

Better *thine* than "yours"; better the singular than the plural when it is the singular that is wanted. There are, as a matter of history, several centuries between *thine* and "yours": the former is Old English, which some call Anglo-Saxon, and the latter is Middle English. Thus, we were saying *thine*, after a fashion, before William the Conqueror came over in that flat-bottomed boat of **isn**. Some of the English, though not so many in the Vale of Evesham, have been saying "yours" for the past five hundred years or so, it is true; but it is not a very long time, as these things go, and I expect we shall hold on to *thine* for a little longer.

### Yourn

Let us not forget *yourn*, either. *Chunt ourn, it's yourn*. Magnificent plurals, *thee knowst*. *Chunt isn, but urn*. Is there any comparable way, outside Latin, of expressing a simple thought so simply?

*Chunt thine, it's mine*. Of these two possessive pronouns, it is curious that one should still be universal and not the other. In the Vale of Evesham, as everywhere else, there is no alternative to *mine*, that very Germanic thing, so ablaze with the pride of possession. But there is something else, *mine tha*.

*Mine tha* is what the pundits call "dialect" because they believe in strait-jackets. Call it what you like, *mine tha* is not to be despised. Treat it rather with reverence, my friends. the Queen's English is a poorer thing without it, *mine tha*.

# More 'Asum Grammar' (27<sup>th</sup> October 1961)

A gentleman from Northleach, Gloucestershire, has written to complain that there wasn't any 'Asum Grammar' in the paper – *"and there wasn't none in last wik's neither."* He says:

> If thee bist going to tell us as Ben Judd's away on holiday, why dussent thee get him back again smartish? We looks forward to Ben Judd, you, and if he yunt thur much longer we shall be talking like a lot of telly announcers. And why cassn't thee get the 'Asum Grammar' printed, so's we could borrow a copy?

Judd hastens to assure his friends that he is not on holiday (except insofar as life is just one long holiday) but simply applying his nose to other grindstones than that of the Grammar. Nevertheless, in acknowledging the support and encouragement of those same friends, he must also hasten to pick up the bait which the gentleman from Northleach has put down.

As a matter of fact, no publisher has ever been invited to publish the 'Asum Grammar' and for this there are at least two reasons: first, it is not finished; secondly, the language of our Vale of Evesham ancestors is not yet a compulsory subject in the schools, not even at evening classes, and when a publisher thinks about grammar he thinks about schools. He cannot consider the subject an economic proposition for sale to the libraries.

Of course, if the gentleman from Northleach (whose name and address we have, but only as a guarantee that there *is* such a person) cared to keep pestering his public librarian for the 'Asum Grammar,' some curious results might follow. Some librarians – for instance, Mr. Huddy at Evesham – pride themselves on being able to obtain any possible book you can name.

There is a limit to this kind of fun, however. A couple of years ago, a completely bona-fide order for the 'Asum Grammar' was placed at a branch shop of the biggest wholesale newsagent and bookseller in the country. The customer was asked to call back (with 15s., if memory serves Judd aright) at the end of the following week. She did so and the reply was that the order hadn't come through, and would she call again in a few days? Patient, long-suffering indeed (necessary virtues for clients of small-town bookshops), the customer did as she was bid. And still there was no book. Eventually she was told it was out of print.

Public libraries (and friends who lend books) *are* a public boon, though, even if they do combine to defeat all but the best-selling popular authors. After all, who will be fool enough to buy a book which he can borrow for nothing, or very nearly so?

No, my friends, there is nothing for it but to continue paying fourpence for the "Journal," wherein all sorts of curious tings have appeared in the past and more may in the future.

# More 'Asum Grammar'

He was neither a mystic nor a fugitive from Stratford, but stood steadily on both feet, and when he said: *I see thy sister up yonder*, he kept his gaze perhaps horizontal, expecting me to do the same. For he understood without illusion, that the lady in question, at that precise moment, was not in sight but in Bretforton, with both feet on the ground. Yet he said: *I see* and what he meant was "I saw." But in the Vale of Evesham the only use a man has for "saw" is to cut wood with, or bones perhaps if he happens to be a butcher. This I understand.

*I see a funny thing th' other day*. It was in the 'Asum Grammar,' that learned work long in preparation but still unpublished. In Volume X (pp.382-794, *et seq*.) there is a vast amount of information about the Evesham irregular verbs. But of these, the verb 'to see' is far and away the most irregular: in fact it is irregular almost to the point of outrage.

Students of linguistic things, and others who know the difference between turnips and mangolds, must now brace themselves to the realisation that the form of the verb 'to see' varies according to whether it is transitive or intransitive. To set out the whole conjugation would be tiresome and unnecessary. In any case, enough is as good as a feast.

| **Verb Transitive** | *Present Indicative* | *I siz* |
| --- | --- | --- |
| | | *Thee sist* |
| | | *Ee siz (Ur siz)* |
| | | *Us siz* |
| | | *You siz* |
| | | *They siz* |
| | *Imperfect indicative* | *I see* |
| | | *Thee sist* |
| | | *Ee see (Ur see)* |
| | | *We see* |
| | | *You see* |
| | | *They see* |
| | *Perfect indicative* | *I a sin* |
| | | *Theest sin* |
| | | *Ee a sin (Ur a sin)* |
| | | *Us a sin* |
| | | *You a sin* |
| | | *They a sin* |

As for the future, pray do not worry about it. *Dussunt trouble thee yud.* (Sufficient unto the day be the evil thereof.) let us now observe the surprising thing.

| **Verb Intransitive** | *Present indicative* | As in verb transitive |
|---|---|---|
| | *Imperfect indicative* | *I sin* |
| | | *Thee sin* |
| | | *Ee sin (Ur sin)* |
| | | *We sin* |
| | | *You sin* |
| | | *They sin* |
| | *Perfect indicative* | As in verb transitive |

Some scrupulous, critical students, accustomed to looking ten times at an object before buying it, may cast doubts upon the existence of a difference here and complain that the machinery of grammar, however lubricated, will not run as far as this. Otherwise, *see* and *sin* are mere alternatives: and this is not so; or, if it is, then they are not equal alternatives. An example or two from ordinary speech, to lift us out of the 'humdrum academicum.'

> *Thee sist that chippa guz-gogs, dussunt?*

> *Aye, I see um yesdy, you.*

> *Astn't thee sinnum, Gertie?*

> *Corse I an't*, etc., etc.

Notice the interrogative variant, with *sin*, but do not let it get you down; and remember, there is no verb more ridiculously irregular than this one. It arouses one's historical curiosity, to wonder what difficulty the Evesham man, our ancestor, encountered (and when) as he was first called upon to see, and to explain what he had seen.

*Ee siz* and *ur siz* (perhaps he thought) so therefore, not to be outdone, *I siz* as well. Likewise, 'you did see' and 'they did see,' so therefore 'I (did) see.' But we shall probably never know. It is all such a long, long time ago. For ever, though, like the convicts who watched their pals jump over the wall, we never 'saw' anything. We just *see*. That is to say, if we are not looking at any object in particular, we just *siz*.

# More 'Asum Grammar' (24th November 1961)

*Cold, yunnit?* The mother's advice to her shivering son, as he trotted home from school the other afternoon, was: *Pull thee yat well down over thee yurs.* His obedience showed his comprehension. And so also must we comprehend. We must get it into our *yuds.* To the foreign visitor, abroad in our paradisal Vale, it is probably rather trying, from time to time, to understand that although we drop our aitches, we do not simply leave it at that, we are induced to drop an aitch and pick up a why. *Come yur, block yud! Cossunt yur what I'm a-tellin tha?* Such language may not be conspicuously polite, but at least it is clear and it is utterly free from any difficulty in spelling. *Theenst spell yur, cossunt?*

Now it is true that not all dropped aspirates are replaced by *y*. One, at least, takes the *w* instead: *wum. Wum* is where the fire is, and slippers, and a comfortable chair, and good books. *Thur's no place like wum. Iger tell if thur is.*

The historical reason why the Evesham man says, for example, *yur* for "hear" or "here," *yud* for "head," and *yup* for "heap," is explored at some length in the 'Asum Grammar,' that learned work so long in preparation and still unpublished. To put it in a nutshell, the situation is that everybody in civilised England would say *yup* for "heap" if their speech had been preserved properly down the centuries. Once upon a time, getting on for a thousand years ago, people would rightly have regarded as a gibbering foreigner anybody who referred to a "manure heap." It is possible that some might nowadays, too, but the point or essence of this particular matter is that if you referred to a *muck-yup* you would have stood a much greater chance of being understood.

In fact, the asthmatic old aspirate, which is so characteristic of England's wheezy old climate, made no improvement whatever to the words to which it attached its parasitic old self. *Yup* (yes, my friends, and *yud* and *yur* as well) is exactly the correct English pronunciation. It is the rare example (the exception, if you like, which proves the rule) where we are right and the rest of the world is wrong. Let us look forward, shall we, to the day when the Mother of Parliaments, which cares so much for spreading the English way of life, shall make a determined effort to spread *yur* and *yud* and *yups* throughout the Commonwealth. Ghana, for instance, could obviously make good use of a few good *yuds.*

But they *yunt chup.* There is another fine word – *chup.* It is such a pity that modern commerce must go out of its way to avoid *chup.* Goods are anything but *chup*, in the Affluent Society. They must be inexpensive, low-priced, reasonable, moderate, or economical: anything but *chup.* It is a word which started as a noun and lost most of its strength when it was turned into an adjective. Nowadays it is an abusive sort of adjective altogether. What a pity, nothing good is *chup!*

# For your book list

*Mine thee fit*, ed. B. Judd (Grist-Bitung, Trincomalee, Rs.13.50)

Here is a Christmas present that is quite different from anything else you will have found in the shops: a concise guide to correct speech in the Vale of Evesham. It is a 'must' for visitors; indeed, it is equally a 'must' for residents with fewer than five generations of Evesham ancestors behind them: to all but the unconsciously adept (or the invincibly inept, as some alien wits would have it), this little pocket-sized volume will form a standing safeguard against the perils of putting their feet in it. Hence the title.

It is especially recommended to those who would compose the rural bits in radio scripts, or drink rough cider in village pubs: people who possess an unshakable conviction that once they move outside their 30-miles-an-hour limit they will meet a farmer called Jarge, who "baint very well heddicated," and all his yokel tribe – buxom, fresh-cheeked wenches; lusty, dim-witted ploughboys; quaint fools, the lot. This will shake them. The motto on the title page is a proverb originated by St. Ambrose about sixteen hundred years ago, though it may well have developed a little since then:

> **SICUTUERIS ESUMAE, ESUMO VIVITO MORE;**
> **SI FUERIS ALIBI, VIVITO SICUT IBI.**

It is splendid advice, printed appropriately in Roman capitals. Underneath, in italics, there is a translation from the Mediæval Latin into the Modern Asum, the first time this has ever been accomplished, but probably not the last:

> *If thee bist in Asum, live like th' Asum folks do;*
> *If thee bist sumwur alss, live like they do thur, you.*

The preface re-clarifies the compiler's position in relation to the study and use of language. It was high time this was done, for the continued publication of what can really only be described as tit-bits from that learned work, long in preparation, but still unpublished, the 'Asum Grammar,' has undoubtedly tended to obscure the character of his work. One had begun to wonder whether the project was intended to be a work of ironic humour directed to an elite, of bucolic jest directed at the faithful, or of serious study The compiler now answers:

> If a grammarian can raise an occasional laugh in the process of demonstrating the rules of language he ought to be grateful and not look to see who is laughing or what the are laughing at. The purpose of the 'Asum Grammar' is to do for the Evesham language what Fowler did for the mother tongue and to defend its purity while there is still time to defend anything. Suaviter in modo, fortiter in re.

'Mine thee fits,' like the parent work, is full of examples which the compiler adduces in evidence for his apparent belief that anything, without exception, can be proved by example. He mentions, for instance, the word *wicked* and pleads that it has no association at all with evil, sin or guilt. He says the meaning of it is entirely subjective in that it can mean whatever the speaker chooses it shall mean.

In proof of this categorisation, which is new to philologists, he tells the story of a printer whose unfortunate task it was to compose in one day a larger number of pages than was considered seemly in the trade. It was a standing-up job and the printer had been doing it for some fourteen and a half hours when the compiler of this volume greeted him. The conversation is transcribed and only one word is said to have been omitted:

> **COMPILER**: *Ow bist dooin, Don?*
>
> **PRINTER**: *My fit be wicked.*

Now, what the present reviewer cannot understand is the nature of the omitted word. The sentence is complete, with subject, predicate and object; and it is a perfectly understandable statement. It is something less than entirely satisfactory if Mr. Judd is going to tell us half a story, miss out the interesting bit and still expect us to laugh.

# More 'Asum Grammar' (9th March 1962)

Hopeful news for those who are interested in our common tongue came this week from the United States with the announcement that the new edition of Webster's Dictionary (the Americans' chief work of its kind) has admitted the word "ain't." Can it be long, now, that the barriers are obviously down, before *yunt* also finds its place among the acknowledged tools of speech? After all, as it has been pointed out, the purpose of Webster's Dictionary is to indicate what is admissible in the way of *written* words; and the American child can now write "ain't" in his schoolwork compositions without fear of correction.

One wonders what the result would be if an Evesham child chose to work *yunt* four or five times into this homework. Perhaps an enterprising one would try it and let me know the outcome?... On the other hand, perhaps it might be better to wait a little, until the Oxford Dictionary has decided which way to jump...

Bridge St
Evesham

# Names of flowers & trees & birds &c.

## *Flowers (and some weeds)*

| | |
|---|---|
| **Bloody-thumbs** | Quaker grass (also called **quakers**) |
| **Bur-dock** | Dock |
| **Crazy** | Buttercup |
| **Dog-daisy** | A wild flower the blossom of which resembles a daisy |
| **Fire-lights** | Violets |
| **Fuzzen** | Gorse or furze |
| **Garden-gate** | Heartsease or pansy |
| **Golden-chain** | Laburnum |
| **Jilly-flower** | Wallflower |
| **Moon-daisy** | Ox-eyed daisy (also called **moons**) |
| **Neddy-grinnel** | Dog-rose briar |
| **Piss-a-bed** | Dandelion (the downy seed head is the **clock**) |
| **Pretty-Betty** | London Pride |
| **Squitch** | Couch grass (also called **scootch**) |
| **Sow-thistle** | Broad-leaved thistle |
| **Tosty-ball** | Cowslip ball |
| **Wave-wind** | Wild convolvulus |

## *Crops & such*

| | |
|---|---|
| **Ails** | Barley beards |
| **Bannits** | Walnuts |
| **Byuns** | Beans (the stubble is **byun-brish**) |
| **Chits** | Shoots from potatoes, wheat, &c. when germination has started |
| **Cone-wheat** | Bearded wheat |
| **Conger** | Cucumber (also called a **cow-cummer**) |
| **Guzgogs** | Gooseberries |
| **Hobli-onkers** | Horse chestnuts |
| **Murfeys** | Potatoes (though typically just called **taters** or **spuds**) |
| **Paize** | Peas |
| **Peasy-pouse** | Peas and beans growing together |
| **Piles** | The beard of barley (detached from the grains with a **piling-iron**) |
| **Scrigglings** | Apples stunted in growth which then ripen before the main crop |
| **Sill-green** | House leek |
| **Sparra-grass** | Asparagus |
| **Turmit** | Turnip |

## *Birds*

| | |
|---|---|
| **Aizac** | Haybird |
| **Biddy** | A chicken or fowl |
| **Black-stare** | Starling |
| **Bolchin** | An unfledged bird |
| **Chate** | Grasshopper warbler (also called **chut**) |
| **Cuckoo's-maid** | Wry-neck (also called **cuckoo's-mate**) |
| **Felt-wing** | Red wing |
| **Glany** | Guinea-fowl |
| **Gull** | Young goose or young cuckoo (*I Henry IV* V.I) |
| **Hedge-betty** | Common sparrow |
| **Hum-buzz** | Cock-chafer |
| **Maggit** | Magpie |
| **Mumruffin** | Long-tailed tit |
| **Pie-finch** | Chaffinch |
| **Quice** | Wood pigeon (also called **quist**) |
| **Stock-eekle** | Woodpecker (also **eekle**) |
| **Tom-tit** | Blue-tit |
| **Squob** | Small unfledged bird |

## *Insects*

| | |
|---|---|
| **Bats** | Beetles |
| **Bree** | Large fly resemble a bee |
| **Breese** | Gadfly (*Anthony and Cleopatra* III.VIII) |
| **Fleen** | Fleas (rare by the 1890s, also flaes) |
| **Hairy-long-legs** | Daddy long-legs |
| **Hod-bow-lud** | Large moth |
| **Horse stinger** | Dragon-fly (also called silver-pin) |
| **Jumper** | Blow-fly maggot |
| **Lady-cow** | Ladybird |
| **Magot-flies** | May flies (*Macbeth* V.I) |
| **Old-maid** | Cattle fly |
| **Piss-aint** | Ant |
| **Rain-bat** | Beetle (apparently if you kill one it will start to rain) |
| **Silver-pin** | Dragon fly (also horse-stinger) |

## *Animals*

| | |
|---|---|
| **Blind worm** | Grass snake (*Midsummer's Night Dream*, II.III) |
| **Ether** | Adder |
| **Fitcher** | Polecat (*Othello* IV.I; *Lear* IV.VI) |
| **Hardi-shraow** | Shrew-mouse |
| **Hob-ferret** | Male ferret |
| **Jack-hare** | Male hare |
| **Jill-ferret** | Female ferret |
| **Josey** | Toad |
| **Moggy** | Calf |
| **Ridgel** | Half-gelded animal |
| **Sherrog** | Two-year old sheep (shear-hog) |
| **Teg** | One-year old sheep |
| **Thave** | Yearling ewe |
| **Tiddling** | Lamb (or other animal) brought up by hand. |
| **Tup** | Ram (*Othello* V.II and III.II) |
| **Urchin** | Hedgehog (*Titus Andronicus* II.III) |

## *Pigs and parts of a pig*

| | |
|---|---|
| **Apun** | Diaphragm or midriff |
| **Boar-stag** | Old emasculated boar |
| **Brim** | Boar |
| **Chine** | A slice of the spine (commonly cut into four or five lengths) |
| **Chittlins** | Entrails |
| **Hilt** | Young sow |
| **Mudgin** | Fat off the chitterlings (also tippit) |
| **Night-cap** | Stomach (also **tom-hodge**) |
| **Porker** | Pig suitable for killing |
| **Scratchuns** | Solid remains when the fat has been melted down into lard |
| **Souse** | Pickled ears and snout |
| **Store pig** | Pig kept for bacon or pork |
| **Swale** | To burn the hair of pig when killed for bacon (porkers are scalded) |
| **Trunkey** | Small, fat pig |

# More 'Asum Grammar'

## More 'Asum Grammar': Our emphatic 'that' (5<sup>th</sup> October 1962)

*That thee bissunt!* The speaker was a mother, to her child, and all the emphasis was on the word *that*. Had the child been older and addicted, as so many always are, to the unfortunate habit of contradiction, he might have retorted, with equal emphasis: *That I be!* To which the reply must inevitably have been a repetitive: *That thee bissunt!*

It is easy for us to take things for granted that we have known in one recognisable and immutable form all our lives. It is better not to take such things for granted. They are worth looking at quite closely now and again. For example, consider our Vale of Evesham emphatic *that*, how useful it is, how economical (like all our ancient pearls of speech) and how necessary: whence did we obtain it and how long ago?

That learned work, long in preparation but still unpublished, the 'Asum Grammar,' hazards a guess (vol. X, Abbreviated Forms, pp.372-498) that the usage has not developed from a longer declaration which began with the words "I knows." It is unlikely that there was ever a time when that harassed mother would have said: *I knows that thee bussunt*: the emphasis must have been on *knows* in such a case, whereas it is obvious that it was always on *that*.

When an Evesham girl says: *That I yunt!* she really does mean "No." It is not a noun clause in the object. That *yunt* is the predicate, total and self-sufficient. There is nothing more to be said…

Or so she thinks. There is more to be said about *that*, however. Its function, in a unique way, is to qualify the verb: as a part of speech it is undoubtedly an adverb, not (as in the Queen's English) a demonstrative pronoun, adjective, relative pronoun or conjunction. It is often found with *never*. *That ee never!* is the most forceful of denials. It answers imperfect allegations, such as *You trod on my foot! – That I never!*

But to deny perfect allegations, such as *You have stolen my wife!* the word *never* is no good: one needs *ant*…. *That I ant!* If the denial must be a really desperate defence to an unanswerable charge, the double negative is employed: *Theest bin a-drinkin my beer! – That I an, never!*

# More 'Asum Grammar' (15<sup>th</sup> February 1963)

*I never sin thee thur, you!* The remark was made by one man to another in Badsey the other day, and I haven't the slightest idea what he was talking about. Two things, however, were apparent: first, that *thee* was heavily stressed, so making the sentiment somewhat pejorative (*ee oughta bin thur, see?*) and secondly that this wonderful Vale of Evesham use of *never* neither dies nor weakens in its use as the years roll by.

Never is a real, full-blooded negative, an absolute in such forms. In the 'Asum Grammar,' that learned work long in preparation and still unpublished, there is a lengthy section devoted to 'Never'; in which the origins of the form, philosophical as well as grammatical, are deeply explored.

Why, a foreigner might ask, does the Evesham man need to say, for instance, *Er never wasn't?* To put the issue beyond doubt, perhaps, or to express an extremely strong hint? The mildest kind of accusation is countered by the sharp reply, *That I never!*: and the reason for this is probably psychological as much as grammatical. But never mind....

> *Er never ud; Ee never did; we never ad; they never sholl* (be slaves... as in 'Rule Britannia'); *I never av; thee assunt never; I ant never; er uddunt never; they mightn't never; er ant never...*

Examples are endless. As for *Thee cossunt never*, well, that is the most arrogant thing an Evesham man (or woman) can ever utter. And the only fit retort is: *Dussunt be sa sure, you.*

# More 'Asum Grammar' (26<sup>th</sup> April 1963)

In the week when the various seats of learning in the Four Shires have begun to be warmed again after the rather cool Easter holidays, it may be appropriate for us to consider (but very briefly) the present state of our endeavour towards a common language. Everybody seems to admit that we ought to have one and (as the recent debate on the virtues of Esperanto indicated) there are those who are prepared to go to considerably lengths to obtain one, even if they have to invent it.

People will say I'm reactionary, if not perverse, if I say that we shall have a common language eventually, when Britain takes her proper place in Europe (for "this is not politics: it's common sense") so I will say something else – and that is, that we in the Vale of Evesham have a common language already, if we care to use it.

Some people do. In Swan Lane this morning, I heard a little boy say: *I yunt gooin*, and I distinctly heard his mother's reply, which was: *Thee bist*. Little episodes such as this indicate two things, at least, and the first is that education doesn't come naturally, it has to be imposed by authority or some external pressure. And not only education, of course. One can imagine Mr. Heath saying: *We'm a-cummin*, and General de Gaulle replying: *No, thee bissunt*.

But it also indicates (as they know already who study that learned work, so long in preparation but still unpublished, the 'Asum Grammar') that uniformity has got a long way to go when it comes to the matter of language.

# More 'Asum Grammar' (31st May 1963)

I have been asked to explain the distinction between *chunnarf* and *yunnarf*, for the benefit of tourists and other foreigners who may be stumbling, in the Vale of Evesham, upon such dialogue as this:

> *Chunnarf cold, yunnit, you?*
> *Aye, I Yunnarf gooin wum quick.*

That learned work, long in preparation and still unpublished, the 'Asum Grammar,' deals at formidable length with the verb 'to be,' to which *yunt*, *yunnit*, *yunnarf*, *yunn-I*, and all similar derivatives belong. *Chunnarf* belongs there, also, despite its wild appearance.

In the small space available here and now, however, it will probably suffice if I say that *yunnarf,* which is an untranslatable Evesham idiom, can be treated as a completely regular verb without the slightest offence to grammar: but the native will always tend to modify it when the subject of the sentence under analysis can be expressed by the neuter and singular personal pronoun. The modification is imposed by the insistent call for brevity, which is not only insistent but progressive. For example, observe this progression:

*I yunt... I yunna gooin... I yunnarf a-gooin...*

Now substitute 'it' for 'I' and what do you get? *It yunt?* Of course not, the word is *chunt. It yunna gooin?* No – *chunna gooin? It yunnarf a-gooin?* The true specimen is:

*Chunnarf a-gooin*

The *chunnarf* usage is fairly rare because its governing element, 'it,' is equally rare, being applied to little else but the weather or Nature. Usually, subjects are either *ee* or *er.* We may be slow, you see, but we are not neuter.

# More 'Asum Grammar' (5<sup>th</sup> July 1963)

*Chunt fur, sir,* the boy said in Badsey when a passing motorist stopped to ask him how fair it was to Littleton. It was a demonstration, at once, of exemplary courtesy and of the living language and I heartily hope the passing motorist appreciated both.

The *fur* has no connection with the skin of certain animals, of course, though it shares a common pronunciation. It is interesting for a number of reasons, not the least of which is that it is an example of a rather late Vowel Shift, that the thoroughly reputable word *fur* should now be pronounced by most people outside the Vale of Evesham as 'far,' rhyming with 'star.' Historically, it is *fur.* Its origins, etymologically, are Old English (*feor*), Old Teutonic (*ferr*), Old Aryan (per Sanskrit, *paras*), which adds up to a pretty respectable family tree, as you will probably agree.

There is a quotation in the Shorter Oxford English Dictionary, "Sum ferrer and sum nerrer," credited to Wyclif. It looks, therefore, as if *fur* became 'far' in many places after the end of the 14<sup>th</sup> century. But not in the Vale of Evesham. Here we are inclined to be somewhat slow to change our habits, and quite disinclined to put on fashionable airs and graces.

As a matter of fact, the standardisation of vowel sounds in English is a very much more recent development than it is sometimes supposed to be. For instance, it is by no means unknown in the Vale, and it is not an indication of 'illiteracy,' to find the word 'clerk' being pronounced *clurk,* as in the American manner. In the 17<sup>th</sup> and 18<sup>th</sup> centuries, fashion imposed the 'ar' sound on a number of words spelt with 'er,' such as 'servant,' 'vermin' and 'swerve.' Nowadays, 'clerk' is about the only one to survive with the 'ar' sound intact, though rustics (in literature, at least, if not in practice) are often observed to call vermin *varmints*. In the Vale, 'ar' has come more slowly than in other places. There are always a few who back the winner of the Durby.

# More 'Asum Grammar' (23<sup>rd</sup> August 1963)

"Her face is badly pitted..." Very unkind, isn't it? But perhaps necessity impels the police to be so ruthlessly accurate in their description of the lady who can help them with their mail train inquiries. "Speaks with an unattractive London accent..."

But what an un-compliment this is! I rather hope that the lady with the badly pitted face that has launched a thousand detectives turns out to be as innocent as Joan of Arc and gets a reasonable opportunity to defend her unattractive London accent.

For my own part, I find all accents interesting, and doubt if any are objectively attractive or unattractive: it depends on the time, place and company in which they are heard, and, to a certain extent, it depends also on the hearer's frame of mind. Frankly, I don't think I should adversely criticise the accent of somebody who had just paid me over £800 in fivers.

The trouble with the provincial urban accents, of course, is that only the people who have already achieved an eminent respectability in spite of them can use them without incurring social disadvantage at the lower levels. The up-and-coming look down upon them; those who aspire most anxiously towards higher status despise most heartily what they conceive to be the tones of their inferiors. In the rural areas, things are different, *mine tha*. It's one of the pleasures of living in the country, *yunnit?*

# More 'Asum Grammar' (18<sup>th</sup> October 1963)

*Cossunt find no conkers?* There are plenty about, for this is the season when the horse chestnut tree sheds its wonderful conkers, each one richly stained and polished with a finish that not even an 18<sup>th</sup> century cabinet maker could hope to rival. Each one, moreover, is not only beautiful to look at but useful to boys – which is a great deal more than can be said of most objects of beauty. You cannot play conkers with anything but conkers: as yet, there is no plastic, all-the-year-round substitute.

Before writing the word *obbly-onkers*, one hesitates for a moment to consider the proper spelling of it, wondering what the correct form should be, what the etymology is, whence the word derives, who we have to thank for it, and when. In fact, the hesitation is not necessary: the word *obbly-onkers* derives, quite simply, from 'conkers'; and we are back where we started... How do you spell 'conkers'?

'Conkers' has nothing to do with 'conquerors,' William of Normandy, Charles the Great, or any such people. The great Dr. Onions, who has recently celebrated his 90th birthday, says in the Shorter Oxford English Dictionary, that 'conkers' was first noticed in 1877 and that it came from the dialect word 'conker,' meaning a snail-shell. (Conch for a shell comes through Latin from Greek.) Dr. Onions says:

> A boy's game, originally played with snail-shells, now with horse-chestnuts, through which a string is threaded, the object being to break that held by the opponent.

Life is full of surprises, and this is an interesting one. One feels sorry for the ancient boys of England, trying to play conkers with snail-shells. They had to put up with these feeble weapons until some time after 1550, in the reign of Edward VI, when a far-sighted anonymous person had the sense to introduce the horse-chestnut into England. Looking back, it is now seen as the most useful event of that reign.

# More 'Asum Grammar' (22nd November 1963)

*I see thy grandfayther last wik,* the countryman in High Street said to a Saturday morning acquaintance, after asking him how he did and the getting the answer: *Very well, thank ya.* Grammatically, the verb is an interesting specimen. The past tense of it either goes into the Perfect or stays pig-headedly in the Present; and one sometimes wonders why. It would have been acceptable if the countryman had said: *I sin thy grandfayther last wik*; in fact, it would have been more strictly in accordance with established Evesham Usage yet it is still quite common to find people, mostly past middle age, who will say; *I see* when they might have said *I sin* or, in the last resort, could have said: "I saw."

Close observation suggests the reasoning behind the discrimination. You will notice that people who say *I see* when they ought to say *I sin* do so with a little unconscious diffidence: more often than not, they are people of an older generation speaking to their juniors. And I fear the worst: that they are trying not to set a bad example, or to show themselves up, as they see it, to the young. Brought up to speak the Evesham Language without inhibition, sent to schools which tried but failed to eradicate it, they feel a little inferior when they find themselves in conversation with younger people whose schooling has produced another effect. Accordingly, since they know that *sin* is wrong and feel uncomfortable with 'saw,' they fall back on 'see.' But what an awful pity.

# It should have been 'const' (24<sup>th</sup> January 1964)

Overheard in an Evesham shoe shop: *They looks all right, you, but I bet thee cossunt gettum on, cost?* Ben Judd says there is an irregularity here… The word *cost* should really have been *const*… the verb being conjugated thus in the present indicative:

| | |
|---|---|
| *Conn-I* | *Connus* |
| *Const* | *Conn-ya* |
| *Connee* | *Connum* |

…all interrogatively. Judd says he hopes the shoes were a better fit, though.

# More 'Asum Grammar': The pronunciation of 'Evesham' (6<sup>th</sup> March 1964)

The argument about the 'correct' pronunciation of 'Evesham,' which has recurred because a broadcaster claiming some sort of inside information, spoke the word like an outsider, will never be satisfactorily concluded by a victory for one school of thought over the others. There is no strictly definable authorised version, for the very simple reason that there is no strictly definable authority in the matter. For who is to lay down the law?

In the 'Asum Grammar,' that long-awaited but still unpublished work which is concerned with the use of words by past and present resident natives of the Vale of Evesham, there is a monumentally comprehensive commentary on the "History of Place Names as suggested by the apparent development of pronunciation" (vol. IX, p.269 *et seq.*).

At the outset it is suggested that the balance of etymological probabilities ought to be weighed as carefully as possible before any consensus of modern usage, if there is one, is considered at all. We shall take notice of what they say on the Badsey bus and in the bar of the Wheelbarrow and Castle, very likely: but not yet. This is because the "accidents of history," if one may employ so unscientific a term in the services of brevity, have to be dated before their effects can be measured properly. In other words, events must be got into the right order.

Tradition and the work of students combine to indicate an 8<sup>th</sup> century swineherd located on a well-watered tract of land almost encircled by a river as the basic element of the name 'Evesham.' After all these centuries, it is hardly surprising that the poor chap's name is unknown. For the matter of that, it never was. All we do know, and that has been from the start, is that he was a swineherd and that he was a poor chap. There is short answer to the claim, if one is made, that his name was Eoves. It is that 'eoves' is nobody's name: it is the genitive singular belonging to the nominative 'eof' which, in Anglo-Saxon (or, as it is more properly known, Old English) means, quite simply, a swine-herd – and nothing more.

The fact that he was a poor chap is really a matter for the ecclesiastical historian, rather than the grammarian, to explore. Pursuing only the etymology of this ancient business, however, we must look at that early form of the town's name, Eoveshomme (which is recorded in Domesday, 1087) and treat its two components first separately and then together: 'Eoves,' of the swineherd, 'Homme,' the meadow land.

Whether it is really a –ham ending need not detain us at this stage since it is, in any case, of no great consequence. What we have to consider is whether the etymological derivation so far is likely to be correct (and the earliest documents known suggest that it is) and then how the name 'Eoveshomme' was pronounced by the Abbot of Evesham, when that dignitary, one Aegelwy, himself an Anglo-Saxon and not a Norman, was asked by William the Conqueror's inspector of taxes to describe the monastic holdings.

Of course this is a tall order. Unfortunately there are no Anglo-Saxons left to tell us the answer; so we must use a little imagination, though not too much, and consult Henry Sweet. Now here it is only decent to place on record that the interpretation produced is subject to a bit of give and take. But if we take Henry Sweet's word for it that the Old English diphthongs were pronounced with the stress on the first element, then 'Eoves' would more or less rhyme with 'Heave us' as a native of modern Birmingham might say it – except that 'us' (to complicate the situation a little further – and, for heaven's sake, why not, now we've got as deeply into it as this?) 'us' would sound like 'uz,' as they say it in Manchester. 'Eoves,' then, sounds like 'Eva's.' Something that belonged to 'Eof' (Eef) was 'Eoves' (Eva's). I fervently hope that this is now clear.

If it is, we must at once proceed further to the realisation that the original sound of 'Eoveshomme' had four syllables, for the final 'e' was not silent until relatively recently in the history of English, and both 'm's were sounded. 'Eva's-hom-muh.'

After that rather dangerous but necessary incursion into the past of a thousand years ago, it will be easier to look at what happened when the language first levelled (in Middle English) and then lost (in Modern English) its inflexions. Professor Wrenn (in Chambers' Encyclopaedia, vol. V, p.302 b) puts its simply:

> ...the placing of the stress-accent as near the beginning of the word as possible has tended to blur and often later to eliminate unstressed final syllables, which tend to be lost in rapid speech.

So we reach, by the time of Shakespeare perhaps, a stage of which Evesham has become 'Eva's-hom,' with three syllables and the stress on the first. It is still important to remember that the vowel sound in the stress-accent is not a pure, straightforward, modern 'ee,' as in tee-hee, tee-hee, if you should happen to feel like laughing in the old-fashioned manner. It is a sound rather nearer to the 'Yeah, Yeah, Yeah' of those distinguished young gentlemen from Liverpool, more power to their elbows, for they are doing more for the English language than any of the kitchen sink playwrights.

Well, then, it follows that 'Eva's-shum' possesses at least as respectable an ancestry as 'Eve-sham'; so there is really no justification for being uppish with those who say 'Ee-vee-shum,' for they are only doing their best according to their lights.

As for the common usage of the place, the people on the Badsey bus and those in the bar at the Wheelbarrow and Castle know perfectly well, without the help of Henry Sweet, that there is only one acceptable way to pronounce the name 'Evesham' and that it the way all honest swine-herds have, from Eof onwards, 'Asum.' Here, at last, you have the correct vowel qualities, the correct stress-accent, and so much more that is down to earth and unpretentious. Asum.

St Egwin's Church Dorrybourne

# More 'Asum Grammar': the verb 'to hurt' (19<sup>th</sup> June 1964)

*Twunt urt*, said the dustman complacently, acknowledging the existence of the dent in the dustbin. And literally he was right. It seemed unlikely that the dent, any dent, in a dustbin at least, could hurt anybody. But that was hardly what the dustman meant. What he did mean, I expect, was: "It's won't matter." And in that respect it was hardly for the dustman to say, for it was not his dustbin that he had dented.

The occurrence of *urt* in the common language of the Vale of Evesham is an interesting example of one short word fulfilling several grammatical purposes. The 'Asum Grammar,' that learned work long in preparation but still unpublished, refers to it in detail, giving examples from ancient and modern usage as transitive verb, intransitive verb, past participle and noun, as well as exploring the history of the stem as far back into its Old French, Celtic, Welsh and Cornish origins as seems decent or necessary.

In its use as an intransitive verb, *urt* means something different from *urt* as a transitive verb. For example, *Twunt urtcha*, which might be said by a dentist who had really determined to master the vernacular, means: "It won't hurt you."

If the same dentist says *Twunt urt*, his meaning is the same: the verb is as transitive as the pain is transient, the object of the sentence being understood.

But if he is talking about a dent in a dustbin, or a job that is not quite perfect or any other sort of blot on an otherwise satisfactory escutcheon, the verb is intransitive. He means that it will not matter. And one wonders why.

Perhaps the explanation is to be found in the sense that hurt can mean mischievous or harmful. *Twunt urt* means, then, "It will not cause mischief or be harmful." The dustman dents the dustbin and comes to the perfectly reasonable conclusion that the dent will not cause any mischief or harm. If the dent becomes a hole, or course, the verb is undoubtedly transitive (and the dustman is a fool).

# More 'Asum Grammar': Book review (1st January 1965)

**Ben Judd, 'Economy of *Aaron*,' Grist-Bitung, Trincomalee, Rs.13.50.**

When I saw this title, I began to wonder whether the present mood of the age we live in, demanding that every fact of life shall be expressed in terms of economics, had gone just a little too far. But the use of both words is, after all (as one should have expected from this author) only literal, and strictly literal. This is neither a work of economics nor an essay in Biblical Exegesis. For this double mercy we may as well be grateful.

The book is, in fact, a commentary on the way in which the Common People of the Vale of Evesham make use of the shortest possible form of words in which to express profound truths by way of ***obiter dicta***: the quotation on the title page is *I ant sin narum* and it is not the slightest use, dear reader (and a happy new year to you!) searching your ever-dimming memories of the classics in order to identify either the source or the language. For if you require the term to be translated and explained to you at all, there is only one course you can take: and that is to read the whole book.

*Aaron* and *narun* are not brothers, though the half deaf might take them for identical twins; actually, they are opposites. For instance, a man might ask another, *Ast thee got aaron?* And might be told, in a disappointing reply, *No, I ant got narun.* Of course, if he was being asked if he had got what happened to be something that he did not want, then he would not be disappointed. And this also is a matter of grammar, if ever so obvious.

*Aaron* and *narun* are the most economical forms, in any kind of English usage, of expressions that are conventional and long-surviving. It will be easier to concentrate on *narun* here: *Ee ant sin narun, er ant ad narun, er don't want narun*, etc. The double negative is completely necessary as Shakespeare knew. The Shorter Oxford Dictionary gives "Ne'er a" as an adjectival phrase with a late Middle English origin, and calls it dialectical or poetical. The translation is "Never a, not a, no!"

In the Evesham Language, however, we progress a stage further that the Oxford Language does, and add *un*. Who can deny that the expression is thereby improved? *Narun*, in two syllables, does the work of three separate words… never… a… one… But if one does more than that: it totally removes the horsey sound for which conventional English is notorious and offers instead a flow of sheer poetry. *If thee knowst a better word, I ant found narun.*

# More 'Asum Grammar': Choice of words (19<sup>th</sup> November 1965)

Anything that can be printed or said can also be seen, says the rash young man on the telly. Those of us who care about the language of the people have news for him. He is wildly wrong. There are words and *words*. Some are in dictionaries. Some are in that learned work, long in preparation but still unpublished, the 'Asum Grammar.' His word is nowhere. It has no etymology, no ancestry, only usage. It is meaningless. If he gets his vocabulary off lavatory walls, as Lawrence did, that is his affair. But if he thinks his word has any definable meaning, upon which he or anybody else has any standing to instruct others, he is not only a rash young man but an ignorant one too. It is not only so-called prudes and puritans who are entitled to suspect his motives.

The changing fashion in words is an interesting thing, as anybody knows who has lived long enough in the Vale of Evesham to notice how people are gradually preferring *yunnum* to *yunt they*.

> *Jack's sprouts be a rare lot, yunnum? – Aye, they be, yunt they?*

Somehow, both expressions are equally acceptable; each has a respectable ancestry; and yet the first is surely more euphonious than the second, and easier to say, without losing any of its significance or grammatical integrity. That is how it always was with genuine language.

There was a time when the universal use was *byunnum*, and this was a beautiful example of linguistic development. It may occasionally be found even today, and the users of it probably regret its gradual supersession. But it has no place on the telly. It can be said, certainly. It cannot correctly be printed, without recourse to phonetic notation; and this is out of the question because only people who have mastered the notation can read as well as write. And how can anybody ever *see* a word? Have you ever seen one? *Ast thee sin one?*

Words make their effect by their sound. That is why *Whurbiss goin?* despite a certain tendency to decadence, in not the inferior of "Where are you going?" As for economy, it is almost the rival of "Quo vadis?" And any language that can stand up to Latin is worthy of anybody's respect. The modern difficulty is that there are too many 'in'-words and 'out'-words. Some that are 'in' ought to be 'out,' and *vice versa*. The real criterion is usefulness. *Woddus think, you?*

The rash young man on the telly will do better to concentrate on the best use of real words, as Shakespeare knew and used them. As for his naughty expression, its correct usage (among fighting men, where it is common) is purely one of poetic emphasis. On the messdecks of warships it is a universal part of speech. On the quarterdecks also. It there ceases to be naughty. It does not mean what the rash young man thinks it means. He was trying, and failing, to be clever.

# More 'Asum Grammar' (25<sup>th</sup> December 1969)

As I was saying, several years ago, the people who have been brought up to speak the Evesham language were always very pig-headed about their past participles.

A simple example, as typical as any is likely to be this side of Christmas, will probably suffice: in (say) 1810 an Englishman who shot a rabbit, damaged a public building, stole a pocket handkerchief, or committed any one of 219 other felonies, was hanged; but in the Vale of Evesham, always supposing he was silly enough to be caught, he was *ung*.

This, however, shall not be an historical dissertation on capital punishment or a wordy commentary on the social benefits thereof; here we shall keep politics and emotion out of it and talk only of the more important and lasting business of grammar.

There is something satisfactory about the simplicity of an all-purpose word such as *ung*. Indeed, there is probably no verb quite as regular as the Evesham verb *to ang*; except in the 2<sup>nd</sup> person present indicative (which ought to be *angst*, in theory, and probably would be if that usage had not been stolen by the Germans) it is all *angs* and *ung*.

> *I angs me at on thuck, you*
> *E angs out is yud*
> *Er angs out the washin*

At least *er* used *tang out the washin* before the introduction of washing machines and launderettes. To continue the conjugation, though.

> *We angs togyuther*
> *You lottangs about too much*
> *They angs on be the skin a thur tith*

Fred Archer can have that one for nothing. Pedantry was always an inescapable feature of this column and so it shall remain. In some primitive villages they may still say *thee angst thee at up*, but, as I say, it has not been heard lately. Anyhow, hatless is the fashion. *Angs out of* is a colloquialism of the lower deck which has no place in a decent newspaper. *Ung* is past and present, passive as well as active. *I ung back a bit.*

> *E ung*            *You lot ung*
> *Er ung*           *They ung*
> *We ung*

The intelligent student will not need me to explain every time precisely what was *ung* and *wur*, or indeed why; but it is necessary to note, again, that the conjugation is deficient of a convincing 2<sup>nd</sup> person: *if theest ever urd a mon (or umman) say ungst*, he or she was probably talking about something else, and in no very complimentary terms either. As for the passive users, there is room for argument if you feel like it.

> *Thy uncle was ung, and if thee bissunt cyurful theelt get ung like thy uncle.*

There was a time, our elders used to tell us, when unkind people would say such things as this to those whom the cap might fit; but they must all have disappeared, *yurs agoo.*

| | |
|---|---|
| *Ida vung* | *Weeda vung* |
| *Eedea vung* | *You lottudda vung* |
| *Erda vung* | *Theyda vung* |

It is not only grammatically but historically true. The hanging of a man for cutting down a cherry tree is on record and, even though it happened in Essex, where cherry trees have always been somewhat thin on the ground, there is no doubt that many of the cases that come before modern magistrates and carry a small fine as penalty, would have been hanging matters not all that long ago.

The Campden Wonder has got to come into this eventually. Mrs. Perry and her two sons were all unfortunately topped for murdering William Harrison (who was alive and well all the time) as every schoolboy knows. The matter has been too adequately aired elsewhere to bear repeating here and now (Sir George Clark, The Campden Wonder, Oxford University Press, is the best of the many works on the subject) and yet there is much remaining mystery. For instance, were the family hanged or *ung*? Sir George Clark, citing some tatty old broadsheets in the Bodleian and the court records (which carry the abbreviation for *Suspenditur*) concludes that they were hanged. The balance of linguistic probability is that they were not suspended, or hanged, or anything fancy; just *ung*.

# More Asum Grammar (20<sup>th</sup> August 1970)

Whatever the outcome of the British application to join the European Common Market, one thing is pretty clear already in the Vale of Evesham supermarkets: if the foreigners want to do business with us, they will have to learn our language.

As I say, it is clear in the supermarkets. It is not enough to carry your wire basket to the check-out desk and be able to pay. If the cashier says, *"Wurbiss gooin?"* you need to have the right answer as well as the right money ready. Ignorance was never an excuse.

In the 'Asum Grammar,' which no visitor to the Vale can afford to be without, *"Wurbiss Gooin?"* and all its relations are carefully explored. Indeed, as well-informed readers of this newspaper are aware, all the conjugations are carried to a degree of sophistication that might make a respectable Latinist give up and take to growing sprouts. In the verb *ta goo*, for instance, the active voice has a present indicative tense of real beauty and subtlety:-

> *Ima gooin*
> *Thee bist a-gooin,* or *Thee bist gooin*
> *Eeza gooin,* or *Erza gooin*
> *Weema gooin,* or *Weemorla gooin*
> *Youma gooin,* or *Yourmorla gooin*
> *Theyma gooin,* or *Theymorla gooin*

Of this there are at least two interrogative forms, called the Nonne and the Num forms. The first expects the answer "yes," as every schoolboy knows, and the second knows there's nothing doing. The Nonne Form:

> *Byoiya gooin?*
> *Stheeya gooin?*
> *Izzee gooin?* or *Izzur gooin?*
> *Beeyussa gooin?*
> *Be you a-gooin?*
> *Be they a-gooin?*

For a reason it is beyond the profundity of a mere grammarian to ponder, the Num form is commoner. (Nevertheless the 'Asum Grammar' does ponder it, in vol.iii, page 429). The Num form:

> *Byunnoya goin, Byuntoi gooin, Yunnoya gooin,* or *Yuntoi gooin?*
>
> *Bissunthee gooin, Yuncha gooin, Byuncha going?*
>
> *Yunneeya gooin, Yunty gooin, Yunna gooin, Byunty gooin, Byunteeya gooin, Yunnera gooin, Yunter gooin, Yuntera gooin, Byunter gooin?*
>
> *Byuntera gooin,* etc. (See Appendix IX, where this is fully worked out, with many illustrations).
>
> *Byunnussa gooin, Byuntussa gooin, Yunnussa gooin,* etc.
>
> *Be you loota gooin,* or *Berra gooin?*
>
> *Beeyumma gooin,* or *Beeyumorla gooin?*

The Italians will certainly face peculiar difficulties and these will probably be treated of later.


*In the letters page (14th February 1974) one R.W. Long of Newlands, Pershore, wondered at the end of a letter: "I have seen no contributions from your expert in the local vernacular. In other words – owlungavvabinjudd?" The Editor kindly added as a footnote: "Judd yunt judd. Iger tell if he is."*

# More Asum Grammar (26<sup>th</sup> December 1974)

*Woddus think thee biss doin?*

The question, asked with a courtesy that was rare even then, used to be the opening gambit of old-fashioned policemen when they wanted someone in the Vale of Evesham to help them with their inquiries. Nowadays, being mostly foreigners, they are somewhat less sophisticated and the question has fallen into desuetude. It survives, however, and monumentally, in that long-awaited yet still unpublished work, the 'Asum Grammar'; and the specimens of usage that now follow are extracts from the appendix to volume VI.

*Wodduss think thee biss doin?* shows the now rare second person singular, and twice at that.

*Wodduss think weema doin?* twice uses the first person plural, in spite of the superficial similarity between *wodduss* and *wodduss*.

Visitors to the Vale of Evesham will probably need to be told that the first *wodduss* means "What dost (thou)?" and that the second *wodduss* means "What do we?" (This distinction between the first person in the subject and in the object is too big a topic to be explored here and now, on an empty stomach). The verb is not really very regular. Purists will say that is because it is not a single verb, but they be safely ignored, having missed the point. Here, conjugated interrogatively, is the person indicative tense of this thing, in the active voice –

> *Woddoo I think I be a-doin?*
>
> *Wodduss think thee biss doin?*
>
> *Woddooee think eesa doin?*

(*Woddooer think erza doing?* has to be added here since the imposition of the statutory equality of the sexes, but it is only common sense).

> *Woddus think weema doin?*
>
> *Wodja think you lot be a-doin?*
>
> *Wodja they think they be doin?*

Careful readers will by this time be wondering whether there is going to be an answer to such questions. Of course there is. There is an answer to everything. These answers, fully amplified, appear in volumes XI and XII, from which extracts may be appearing soon.

# Yet more 'Asum Grammar' (17<sup>th</sup> July 1975)

*Wurbissgooin?* It is the quintessential, fundamental, essential question and there is not always an answer to it. To be sure, there are many possible answers (which are cunningly contrived alternatives) in that long-awaited and still unpublished work, the 'Asum Grammar.' Here and now, the question is asked –

> *Wurby I a-gooin?*        *Wurby uss a-gooin?*
> *Wurbissgooin?*         *Wurby you lot a-gooin?*
> *Wurzargooin?*          *Wurby they a-gooin?*
> *Wurzurgooin?*

The interrogative form of the continuous present tense takes due account of women's rights, as you will see, for this work is frightfully up to date. The answer, if you keep your eyes open, is always that we shall see.

# More Asum Grammar (14<sup>th</sup> August 1975)

*Yunnitot!* It is a pure rhetorical question, hence the exclamation instead of the question mark. For indeed, there is no doubt about it. *Yunnitot.*

This *yunnit* usage, which is common in one form or another wherever English is spoken, is not always rhetorical in the Vale of Evesham. Sometimes it calls for a straight answer and especially when it is in the form *yunnee* or *yunner*; and not in the neuter *yunnit. Yunnee gooin* or *yunnee cummin,* for example, require yeses or noes. An indecisive or hesitant answer invites judgement:

> *Eedunno whether eeza a-cummin or a-gooing*

Or, for the matter of that:

> *Erduna whether erza cummin or gooin.*

And that judgement is unfavourable, not only grammatically. The whole stupendous business is exhaustively explored in the chapter headed 'Nonne' in volume three of that long-awaited and still unpublished work, the 'Asum Grammar.' *Yunnuss* and *yunnum* questions are nearly always true 'Nonne' specimens, we learn. If someone asks you, *Yunnuss lucky?* the proper answer is not 'No' but *'Aye but...'* Similarly if you ask someone *Yunnum a rotten lot?* you do not expect to be disagreed with, otherwise you would never have asked the question. The conjugation is beautifully regular:

> *Yunney*             *Yunnuss*
> *Yuncha*           *Yuncha*
> *Yunnee (yunner)*    *Yunnum*

There is a slightly more emphatic form in those areas of the Vale which lie close to the hills.

| | |
|---|---|
| *Byunteye* | *Byunnus* |
| *Byuncha* | *Byuncha* |
| *Byuntee (byunter)* | *Byuntum* |

On occasion these beautiful words will effectively stand alone and will not easily be withstood. Some grammarians might call them rhetorical and indeed they strictly are; but their strength is their severe antiquity. Far from merely requiring an answer, *byuntey* (properly used) will brook none. Such matters shall shortly be further and more largely investigated.

# More 'Asum Grammar' (25<sup>th</sup> December 1975)

Competent theologians of the old school (who are nowhere near as thick as the Pershore theologians of the new school) will tell you there are two sorts of sin, original and actual. Grammarians will tell you something quite different. There is perfect sin, for one thing. In that immense work, long-awaited and still unpublished, which the civilised world has come to know as the 'Asum Grammar,' there is much said by way of example as well as precept about *sin* – perfect, imperfect and pluperfect. For example, in volume IV on page 192 we find the following jolly conjugation:

| | |
|---|---|
| *I a sinner* | *Us a sinner* |
| *Theest sinner* | *You a sinner* |
| *Ee a sinner* | *They a sinner* |

The sin there is as perfect as perfect can be. It is so also when the object is masculine, neuter or plural. For example:

*I a sinnim, Theest sinnim, Ee a sinnim, Us a sinnim, You a sinnim, They a sinnim.*

*I a sinnit, Theest sinnit, Ee a sinnit, Us a sinnit, You a sinnit, They a sinnit.*

*I a sinnum, Theest sinnum, Ee a sinnum, Us a sinnum, You a sinnum, They a sinnum.*

There are two interrogative uses of this form and both are regular. One is more or less direct and the other requires an affirmative answer unless its two syllables are accented collusively, in which case a negative answer is expected unless the person addressed is deaf, stupid or downright hostile.

| | |
|---|---|
| *Ast thee sinner* | *Uvver sinnim?* |
| *Theest sinner, assunt?* | *Urra sinnim, anter?* |

There is a great deal more to say about all this.

# More 'Asum Grammar': Devolution and the Vale of Evesham (23<sup>rd</sup> December 1976)

**B. Judd (ed.), <u>Self-Government for Uffnum and Other Places, a symposium</u> (Grist-Bitung, Trinco-malee, Rs. 17.50)**

What's sauce for the goose is sauce for the gander, as Mr. Roy Jenkins says in his foreword to this useful book. If the Scots and the Welsh can have it, then might we well have it in Uffnum, and Other Places. *There yunt much to stoppum having it in Asum, you*, he concludes, showing not only how reasonable he is, but also, very nearly, how polyglot.

And of course he is right. As the late Warden of Wadham used to say, *thee cossunt stoppum having it if they wants it, if they knows what they wants and wurta get it.* Of course it all depends on what they wants, and knowing what they wants.

Here we come to the nub of the matter. Nationality depends weightily on language. If the man on the Clapham omnibus and *thummun as a just missed her last bus wum* can truly be said to speak the same language, so be it; but if not they are foreigners to each others, members (as Mr. Heath used to say before they shut him up) of Two Nations. Several contributors favour federation but Mrs. Thatcher is not one of these:

> *Iger tell* [she writes]. *Iger tell if they knows if they be a-cummin or a-gooin. Federate? Iger tell if they ull, so thur.*

Devolution is an ugly word, if not quite the ugliest in this book, and half the difficulty of discussing it lies in the fact that no two people take it to mean quite the same thing. A consultant etymologist retained by the Ministry of Agriculture throws a little light in the right direction: it means he says, "rolling down, descending or falling with, or as with, a rolling motion." He has stolen that, without acknowledgement, from the Oxford Dictionary.

> *But wurbiss rollin down to, O Asum, O Badsey, O Littleton, and what's thad as makes tha want a roll?*

Etymology alone does not tell us whether, when something rolls, it rolls forwards or backwards. The mechanical sciences might have something to say about this but they have not been asked. All we can see from the evidence is that it rolls 'Downhill', indeed it could scarcely roll 'Uphill' without some form of propulsion. Only old Father Thames keeps rolling 'Along'.

The only lesson to be learnt from this astonishing book is one which the elect had always understood, that wogs start half-way across Bidford Bridge, as like as not.

# Bullocking in Badsey: Yet More 'Asum Grammar' (3$^{rd}$ February 1977)

As steadfast readers of long-standing well know, there is no lack of topicality in the successive volumes of that learned work, the 'Asum Grammar.' Bullock, as we see in a long foot note on page 494, where the reference is to 'Terms of Abuse Current in the Littletons', is not in the least abusive when it is simply a noun of singular number, all its offence being in the plural, yet it is capable of meaning many different things.

For example, there is the established difference of viewpoint between them *azzaz* and *azzant*, and it is not for any mere grammarian to say what the late Vice Chancellor *azz* or *ant*, though when one saw him in the Sheldonian not all that many years ago, pontificating in all his finery, he seemed to have plenty. The subject of the simple common noun, however, *ant* got nothing at all.

In Badsey it is a verb as well, though not a very regular one: the conjugation, as far as it goes, is set out pedantically on page 495. But here is the topical point. The 'Asum Grammar' apparently sees no difference between workers and directors, as long as they all work sometimes and preferably in more or less the same direction. As for the verb 'to work', it has less to do with industrial democracy than plum jerkum, for if the latter will not work it will not jerk, and that is that, democracy or no democracy. The serious reader is preferred to the lucid chapter on Privilege and Power, with its explanation of such usages, as *Thee cossunt, Thee dussunt*, et cetera.

# More 'Asum Grammar,' continued

*Werds matter.* The right words in the right order matter greatly: Virgil knew it, Cranmer knew it, Milton knew it, and the woman on the Badsey bus knows it. *Wurst bin?* She asks, and when he tell her she replies *Igertell if thee assn't!* It would be meaningless in Macclesfield.

Leaving aside for a moment the staggering economy of that enormous other, which a pedant might translate as "May I go to hell if thou hast not!" (without thereby making any sense of it at all), let us look more closely at the question, *Wurst bin?*

In an appendix to volume ix of that long waited but still unpublished work, the 'Asum Grammar,' it is held that there is no other European language, classical or modern, in which it is grammatically possible with comparable succinctness to ask someone where he or she has been, though it is conceded that a few may have more graceful ways of doing it.

The form is not invariable. *Wurrust thee bin?* for instance, singles out the person addressed as if he or she has been somewhere disreputable, or is simply late. These second person singular forms of the auxiliary verbs survive strongly in the traditional language of Evesham, while elsewhere they are long since dead and buried, written off as 'arch.' or 'obsol.' even by the great Oxford English Dictionary. England lost a lot of poetry when it abandoned the second person singular, especially its interrogative form in the perfect tense. The French and the German wisely kept theirs, and so did Evesham. *Wurst bin? Cossunt remember? Dussunt tell?*

*Igertell it thee assn't!* In the usage, the first element is syntactically integral. *Well igertell!* can stand by itself, as an expression of astonishment. *Woddus say, theest yut the lot? Well igertell!* Et cetera. But *Igertell if thee assn't* is a very different kettle of grammatical fish. Not only is it undoubtedly an oath, complete in its canonical content, so to speak, but it functions over a negative as it were: in simple terms it asserts something which is not. A lost or ailing language? *Igertell if it is!*[††]

# More 'Asum Grammar' (14th August 1980)

Arrangements seem to be in progress, behind sound-proof doors, for a Papal visit to England. Our Vatican-watcher has two things to say about it at this stage: first, it looks like a now or never chance for St. John Henry Newman (whose claims are every bit as good as any foreigner's), and secondly that if John-Paul II sets his adventurous foot anywhere between Wickhamford and Church Lench, one of his domestic prelates had better have in his briefcase appendix VI of that long-awaited and still unpublished work the 'Asum Grammar.' Not that His Holiness's formidable linguistic powers are likely to be all that easily strained; but if somebody asks his *woddee wanser yut* or *were wanser goo*, or (more directly) *Wodduss myun you?*, the indefatigable Pontiff will want to maintain his 100 per cent record, and give a Straight Answer.

*Wurbiss gooin, worse tha bin, oo said thee cossunt*, and suchlike little questions all figure in this appendix, together with the complete conjugation of the irregular Asum verbs and the declension of the personal pronouns. Since it is possible that the Pope may come in May, there is a helpful footnote about Grass, how it should be grown, cooked and *yut*: and there is a quite helpful biographical bit about John Wesley, included in case His Holiness should run true to form with his unsurprising surprises and find good cause for canonising that great man.

---

[††] The following week (27th December 1979) A.S. Hancox from Bourton-on-the-Water wrote a letter to the *Journal* expressing a common thought: "It is with the greatest pleasure that I read Ben Judd in today's *Journal* and only wish I could look forward to regular examples of Asum Grammar each week in 1980." The published letter was subtitled: *'Wodduss myun, every wick?'* SBB

# More 'Asum Grammar' (2<sup>nd</sup> October 1980)

Since the last prophetic bit of Asum Grammar appeared on this page, it has been announced that the Pope will indeed come to England. Watch this space, as ever, for inside information. We were talking, if you remember, about the peculiar need to arm the polyglot pontiff with a few well-chosen vernacular phrases should he venture into the Vale of Evesham at asparagus time. Space then ran out, as ever. If you are still awake we will start again.

The conventional greeting is *Owbist?* and His Holiness will find this makes sense at any time of the year between Murcot Dock and Bidford Bridge. It is a bit like "How d'ye do" or "Ça va?" or, if you insist on a respectable Roman equivalent, "Salve!"

Now, the expected response to *Owbist?*, whether you are the Pope or the indigenous native, is: *All right you, owbiss thee?* and not *Pretty middlin* or *Me fit are killin me* or anything hypochondriacal like that, unless there is a real difficulty crying out for papal mediation. The conversation thus happily begun, may then continue: *A how's the missis, blesser cotton socks?* to which the straight response is: *Fairter middlin thee knowst* or some such innocent pleasantry. That is a papal question not a papal answer.

# More 'Asum Grammar': a few searching questions (2<sup>nd</sup> July 1981)

*Chunnarf chilly, yunnit?* The words ring out upon the silence, like the opening of a great drama. The response is equally clear: *Yunnit!*

*Chunnarf, yunnarf, yunnit, yunnoi, yunter* and *yuntum* figure colourfully among the interrogative forms of the verb 'to be' in the appendix to volume IV of the 'Asum Grammar,' that long-awaited but still unpublished work which first saw a slight inkling of daylight on this page 25 years ago.

For readers whose first acquaintance with the ancient language of the Vale of Evesham is fewer than 25 years old, some slight explanation is probably due. But not much: they must take us as they find us, and work hard at it. The *arf* element is fairly easy, so we will deal with that first.

*Arf* is synonymous, though not precisely equivalent in mathematical terms, with 50 per cent. Foreigners, for instance, have 'better arves,' 'arf a mo' and 'timenarf.' This is not quite their kind of *arf. Chunnarf chilly*, to be brutally pedantic about it (taking a few grammatical risks into the bargain) means it is considerably more than 50 per cent chilly isn't it? And it is a question which (as another noble language also does in similar circumstances) demands the answer *aye*, rather emphatically. To answer 'no' is a course which cannot be safely taken. So much for the *arf*. We hope it is perfectly clear.

*Chunnarf* might sometimes be rendered as *chuntarf*, implying an apostrophe …'t. *Yunnarf*, however, has the neuter pronoun <u>understood</u>, as we used to say. This will be perfectly plain everywhere except in the University of Cambridge, where an attempt to introduce grammar and analysis has lately failed. Let us pass quickly on to *yunnit, yunnoi, yunter, yunnee,* and *yuntum* or *yunnum,* and note the felicity of the usage in terms of sheer euphony before we probe its depths. The Queen's English is a frail creature in comparison: is it not, am I not, is she not, is he not, are they not! Did you ever hear anything so teutonically cacophonous?

*Chilly, yunnit? A-sat in the warm, yunnoi. Three sheets in the wind, yunnee?* Perfectly comprehensible, *yunnit?* The ready student can now do it effortlessly for himself, *carnee* or *carner?* Let us stick to one verb at a time, though. In the perfect and future tenses of the verb 'to be,' the interrogative forms seem to be depressingly regular:

> *wuzzoi, wust, wuzzee, wuzzer, wuzzus, wuzzum;*
> *wuzznoi, wussunst, wuzznee, wuzzner, wuzznus, wuzznum.*

The future, well not – that is not for today. But it will come.[‡‡]

# More 'Asum Grammar' (22nd October 1981)

Reading the silly story of the Almonry chimney-stack, and visualising the redoubtable Mr. Henry King spreading the efficacious cow dung over it, reminds me that in all old buildings of that sort the doorways tend to be a bit on the low side and so it is sensible to put a little notice up saying: *Mine thee yud.*

Leaving aside the cow dung for another day, though well-informed friends say it needs to be as fresh as possible and preferably steaming, let us look at this *yud.* It has something in common with *yup* (as in a *yuppa* cow dung, or words to that effect) and likewise with *yur* – but not with *thur* or *everywur.*

In other words it is a residual, if not original, aspirate. There is a profound essay upon this very problem in that learned work, long awaited and still unpublished, the 'Asum Grammar'; from which it appears that our rude forefathers in the Vale did not drop their aitches: they never had any. The aspirated aitches in the Queen's English is a quite modern phenomenon. There is nothing at all modern about the traditional Evesham language.

---

[‡‡] The following week (16th September 1982) A.S. Hancox, from Bourton-on-the-Water, wrote to the *Journal* saying: "Sir, May I say what a pleasure it was to find Ben Judd and 'More Asum Grammar' again last week, and in such excellent form. I only wish you could persuade him to favour us more frequently." SBB

It ante-dates all orthography, which is another way of saying it is a language of illiterates (if that is how you really feel about it) for the 'y' we use is a mere phonetic symbol, not the old English 'yog.' And therefore, to digress yet farther (for where is the harm in it?) the 'ye' you sometimes see at Ye Olde Inne must always be pronounced 'The,' because 'yog' sounded 'th...' Is it not wonderful what you can get for 16p[§§]?

Talking about *yuds* (which includes schoolteachers of both sexes) you may sometimes be told that if there were any grammatical consistency in this world *thee yud* would be rendered *thy yud*. Nonsense. The word goes back beyond the Great Vowel Shift, before the 'oi' sound had been heard in this green and pleasant land. The affirmative 'aye' is a very different kettle of fish, to which we shall eventually return.[***]

# More 'Asum Grammar' (9th September 1982)

All this speculation about the mysteries and provenance of Jerkum[†††] inevitably leads the curious to an appendix in volume six of that long-awaited but still unpublished work, the 'Asum Grammar,' wherein many such matters are made clear. Be patient, dear reader, these things are worth waiting for. This little appendix discusses the various uses of the verb 'to work' of which there are many, but only one concerns us today – *Itsa workin you* and *Ittul worktha*.

Now any self-respecting grammarian can see at a glance that *Itsa workin you* is a very intransitive sort of verb, and that *Ittul worktha* is as transitive as you can get, *you* being the object as you will soon find out, if you take too much of it too soon. But not too fast, not too fast, we must not confuse the foreigner. If we say *Itsa workin you* we need look to Latin: that 'you' is the vocative case; it not the object of the sentence; and the subject is the Jerkum. The predicate indicates fermentation – and that is the secret. It is easy when you know how.

Advanced students will of course know without thinking about it: *Ittul worktha* has a verb in the future tense. Experience of Jerkum suggests that it is not that, for into the future that *Ittul worktha*; but let the cobbler stick to his last: this is grammar, not a do-it-yourself book. *Itsa workin you* refers to the Jerkum and what is happening to it and what is happening to you. *Thee seest yur it workin!*

---

[§§] The price of the *Evesham Journal* in 1981. SBB

[***] George Wilson (from Henley-in-Arden) wrote to the *Journal* the following week (27th October 1981): "Sir, When will Ben Judd condescend to advise us of the completion of his long-awaited, learned exposition on Asum Grammar? Meanwhile, I suppose we must be content with this lurid descriptions of the muck-flinging exploits of the estimable Henry King." SBB

[†††] I'm afraid I was the guilty party in this, being then a wine-making seventeen-year old who wrote letters asking about Jerkum to the *Journal* (this one published 19th August 1982). SBB

# More 'Asum Grammar': Well, thee bist, bissunt? (7<sup>th</sup> October 1982)

When it comes down to brass tacks, the spoken word may have its uses but for sheer authority the Printed Word leaves it standing every time. For example, take this matter of *thee*. Gauche young broadcasters and game young politicians often say *thee* when all they mean is 'the.' Even when they have heard you the first time, they often say *ay* when all they mean is 'a.' And here are the seeds of endless confusion, especially in the Vale of Evesham, where people only say *thee* when they mean *thee, you,* and only say *ay* when they did not hear you or are not very interested.

*Thee* is closely examined analytically and descriptively in the first volume of the 'Asum Grammar,' where it appears in a form which is calculated to surprise foreign grammarians. The present indicative of the verb 'to be' is printed thus:

| | |
|---|---|
| *I be* | *Weem** |
| *Thee bist* | *You be* |
| *Eez* or *erz* | *They be** |

Never mind the asterisks, at least for the time being: they refer to the incidence of certain exceptions; but keep watching this space. Today we are looking only at *thee*. *Thee bist* the discriminating reader. *Thee*, in Asum, is the second person singular form in the nominative case and not, as strangers might innocently assume, in the dative or the ablative. *Yur thee assunt gotta thou, theest only gotta thee.*

An ancient Roman or a modern Frenchman would say 'tu es' and mean much the same thing but anyone who has ever dabbled with the horse language of the Saxons would remember that they say 'du bist' and mean precisely the same thing. Not everyone between Childswickham and Bidford Bridge has yellow hair and blue eyes but every time you hear one of them say *thee bist*, hold not the slightest doubt where his ancestors came from, well over a thousand years ago, and there's continuity for you. If he says *thee bissunt*, of course, the grammatical problem is of a different order, and it is not for today...

# More 'Asum Grammar' (17<sup>th</sup> February 1983)

*Chup, chupper, chuppest.* The comparison of adjectives, in any language, needs to be got right. The slightest slip here marks the speaker as a foreigner. As the serious student will discover, such matters as these are meticulously analysed in the Usage sections of that learned work, long in preparation but still unpublished, the 'Asum Grammar,' about which there is nothing *chup*.

A thousand years ago or so, the word in its nominative case simply meant a market: thus were founded 'Chupside' in the City of London, 'Chuppin Campden' in the county of Gloucester, 'Chuppin Norton' in county of Oxford, and various other 'Chuppins' in the little market towns that were first settled by the Saxons, including 'Chuppin Sodbury,' 'Chuppin Ongar' and so on. But *chup*, *chupper* and *chuppest* are phenomena of the present day, not mere dead relics of the Heptarchy.

*Chup* is a relative term, of course, leaving aside the description 'chup and nasty' (see Pejorative Terms, vol. vi, pp.231-342) *chup* on its own presupposes the existence and acknowledgement of a norm. For example, if 100 is the norm, 99 is *chup*, 98 is *chupper* and 97 is *chuppest*, whatever the currency. Likewise 101 is dear, 102 is dearer and 103 dearest. The thing, by its nature, is qualitative.

But beware. *Chup-jacks* do not really sell *chup*: their wares only look *chup*. *Chuppest* is only superlative in simple grammatical terms. In value it will often turn out to be dearest. From such bones is paradox made. Nothing worth anything could ever be got on the *chup*.

# More 'Asum Grammar': Fust thing fust (3<sup>rd</sup> March 1983)

*Fust* is a wine-cask, or a stale musty smell, or the shaft or a column, or the ridge of the roof of a house, or (as an intransitive verb) to become mouldy or stale-smelling, or to taste of the cask. So says the Oxford English Dictionary, but don't you believe it. In the *fust* place, as anyone knows who lives in the Vale of Evesham, there is all the world of difference between *fust* and 'fusty.'

In the *fust* place or 'In principio' (as St. John begins his Gospel) you can take it for granted that there is a great deal more to be said. According to that learned work, long in preparation but still unpublished, the 'Asum Grammar,' *fust* shares with *fuzz* and *bust*, and one or two other words, the quality of being able to manage quite well without the rolling 'r' which means so much to the comfort of the Scots and the Italians.

Other people will go on calling the spiny evergreen shrub 'furze bush,' but the Evesham speaker calls it *fuzz*, which has nothing to do with the police. If anything flies asunder anywhere in England it bursts, but in Evesham it *busts*. *Fust* things *fust*, then. If it *busts* it deserves to be *cussed*, especially if it happens to be a *puss full of money you*.

# More 'Asum Grammar' (10<sup>th</sup> March 1983)

There's more in this than meets the eye, *mointha*. In the 'Asum Grammar,' that learned work long in preparation but still unpublished, the etymological use of *mointha* will be found early in chapter 6 of volume iv, in the section headed 'Emphases.' There it is explained that the emphatic charge of *mointha* depends not on the ideas of the person who is speaking but on the responses of the person who is being spoken to. Thus, one who says there is more in this than meets the eye, and leaves it at that as something evident and obvious.

But if the person being addressed is sceptical, or obtuse, or thick, or needs convincing of the perfectly obvious (which amounts to the same thing) then the speaker throws in a *mointha* or two. No other language with Latin or Teutonic ancestors has a *mointha*. The Scottish 'd'ye ken' is close but not linguistically. The French 'voyez-vous' likewise. There is much more to it than meets the eye, *mointha*.

# More 'Asum Grammar': Advanced Studies (9<sup>th</sup> June 1983)

------- *Thee knowst*. It is a time-honoured response by an Evesham native, rendered with a knowing smile, for who asks a silly questions may not take a silly answer.

> *Oobist you vote for? – Thee knowst.*
> *Ow many makes five? – Thee knowst.*

The response has a great deal to do with knowledge, and that of the kindest kind, but precious little to do with grammar, and so it's found among the Dialect Forms in volume vi of the 'Asum Grammar,' and requires a little explanation. Superficially, the usage is akin to the Authorized Version, 'thou knowest,' which looks similar to *thee knowst*. But it is necessary in these matters to be very careful: and to note that the AV 'thou' is the second person singular personal pronoun in the nominative case in the Queen's English, and that (on the face of it) the Evesham *thee* is in the accusative. There is certainly a mistake here somewhere, perhaps you thought? Yet it is clear that they must be the same thing, near enough. Somewhere in the lost forgotten centuries, it looks as if someone forget to tell the folks of Evesham about the Vowel Shifts, and the common man of the Vale also never adopts the archaism of making two syllables of *knowst. Now thee knowst, dussunt?*

*Thee cossunt* find anywhere in the Vale anyone who says 'thou,' unless he is a fugitive Yorkshireman, an honest Quaker, or a churchman desperately committed to the language of the late Archbishop Cranmer. *Thee cossunt, cost?* The grammatical question is easy... *If thee cossunt, why dussunst?* But of course it is right as well as decent to be as clear as possible to willing students, so we will stoop to a feeble translation:

> *Cossunst* – canst thou not?

> *Dussunst* – why is it that thou cannot?

But perhaps *thee cossunt (thee knowst)* and in that case your ignorance is merely feigned. Perhaps *thee dussunst*? Well, then, why not? There is an awful difference between *cossunt* and *dussunst*, which we will perhaps discuss another day, but in the meantime, let us get back to the point. *Wobbiss dooin?* – *Thee knowst.*

# More 'Asum Grammar': Evolution of Down Thur (18th August 1983)

*Yur, thur, anywur, everywur, up yur, down thur, from yurtur thur...* it is a long way on a hot day. Whether it is a demonstrative adverb, a relative or conjunctive adverb or a plain substantive, and under which circumstances, can be investigated, another day, at enormous length, in great detail, with copious illustration. Here and now, *yur and thur*, let us contemplate the substantive form alone, patient readers, for it is incomparably topical and important.

According to the 'Asum Grammar,' that learned work long in preparation, long-awaited but still unpublished, *down thur* was a large building in Avonside[‡‡‡] and it was the prudent purpose of working people getting on in years to keep out of it. Nobody wanted to go *down thur*. It was not exactly a fate worse than death: it was death, with knobs on.

Nor did the passage of the National Health Bill in 1948 allay one whit the deep-seated fear of the honest and industrious elderly about going *down thur*. The term is no longer heard how, the very idea is expressed nowhere in print (except in a historical footnote buried quietly in volume v of the 'Asum Grammar') and the compiler would now resurrect it now, but for the crying need: the Big Brothers are up to their devious tricks, and they must be deterred. It is abundantly clear that the vast majority of young mothers in the Vale of Evesham wish to go to Avonside to have their babies.

Carping readers of the disagreeable sort may well wonder what the having of babies has got to do with going *down thur*. They, like the rest of us in this Vale of Tears, must be patient. The irony of it is that these young women's great-great-grandmothers were dead set against going *down thur*, yet the present generation wants to go *no-wur else*. The irony, like all ironies, is of life and death. We shall return to it, *yur, thur* and *everywur*.

---

[‡‡‡] The local aversion to Avonside Hospital may in part be explained by the fact that it had previously been the workhouse. SBB

In the
Market
Place
Evesham

# What makes the 'Asum' character?

*Abridged from Philip Beck's article from the Evesham Journal (31<sup>st</sup> May 1957)*

Have you ever thought how we Evesham people have certain characteristics that distinguish us from our inhabitants of other places? Of course, we are not like a flock of sheep, thank heavens. There are those with brains and those without; those who talk 'Asum' and those who talk English. But after a lifetime of mingling with our townsfolk, people of many other towns, at home and abroad, we have come to the conclusion that the people of Evesham are unique.

In the first place, let's be frank, there is no true aristocracy in the town; no titled families with centuries of tradition behind them. In fact, no matter what may be our income group, no matter whether we come from Greenhill, Bengeworth or Fairfield, most of us are descended from peasant stock. But that's nothing to be ashamed of, if you don't like the word 'peasant,' substitute 'hard-working men of the land,' and be proud of it.

Many families owe their present comfort to the sweated labour and, in many cases, astute foresight of their ancestors. Those men knew how to cultivate the rich soil of the Vale to the best advantage and they passed on their skill to their sons. With the passing of the years successive families have improved on the methods, until today there are many big businesses based on very humble origins. Certain 'visitors' during the war years called the Evesham people 'Cabbages,' and they retaliated by calling them 'Blight.' But the 'visitors' should have realised that we cabbages are as skilled and as important to the nation's existence as atomic scientists, engine drivers or factory workers.

Our speech, as we have already indicated, varies. To some ears, the 'Asum' dialect is appalling and, in spite of the high standard of English teaching in the local schools, there is no sign of its being on the wane. The trouble is that whereas it may be impressed on a scholar that it is 'hwhere' and not *wur* and 'she isn't' instead of *'er yunt*, the good work is soon undone by his family, with whom he spends most of his time.

It is probable that the English teachers have given up trying to teach these children to speak correctly. It must be a formidable task. In our Grammar School days the teachers tried hard, but it was a hopeless business. *Oo wants ter speak posh anyway?* seemed to be the attitude of many pupils.

So the 'Asum' dialect seems to be here to stay, and we must accept it as one of the chief characteristics of the town. Yet we would not support the contention that it is 'appalling.' In our opinion, the speech of the people of certain other parts of the country is much worse. Take Birmingham, for instance. "Are yow going down the Pairshore Rowd to get some wairms for the bairds?" is far harsher to our ears than *If I'd a know'd thee wasn't agooin' I 'ouldn't a went.*

The Scots and Welsh speech, on the other hand, is much softer and more musical. 'Asum' is rough, some might call it 'quaint,' but it's not that bad.

And, of course, there are hundreds amongst us who do speak English as it should be spoken, which does not mean the refined accent adopted by a few who mistakenly believe that it elevates their social status. We prefer 'Asum' to 'Oxford.' At least, it's honest.

Now let's consider what Evesham folks talk about. The main topics appear to be the weather, the crops and other people's affairs. The first and third of these subjects are, of course, national rather than local characteristics. We certainly have a strong sense of humour, but, unfortunately, our wit is tending to become second-hand. Original humour is giving way to recaps on jokes seen on television or heard on the radio. This is much to be deplored. Real humorists, great rollicking Dickensian wits, are hard to find these days. We have only met one in the past. He was a bus conductor, and much of his humour bordered on the obscene.

We are not very hospitable. Newcomers to the town do not find it very easy to get to know Evesham people. Some complain that they have lived in the town several years and have yet to break the ice with their neighbours. But this is perhaps a regional rather than a local failing. It is well known that friendliness and hospitality is more freely dispensed as one moves to the north. We are not as aloof as the folks further south, but we certainly haven't the 'Ello Luv' warmth of the northerners.

Of course, it is fatal for the newcomer to underestimate the Evesham man, to regard him as an intellectual and social inferior just because he has a queer way of talking. That was the mistake of the wartime billetees. Genuine friendship and understanding helps a lot towards 'getting in' with the Evesham people.

So far as dress is concerned, well, let's be honest again, the majority of Evesham people are badly dressed. The women seem to prefer 'sensible' to fashionable attire. The female dress parade in the streets is drab. There are far too many unbecoming red, brown and green outfits, fitting where they touch. Yet this is surprising when one notices the attractive clothes displayed in the dress shops in the town. The question is, "Who buys them and were do they wear them?"

One theory is that local women only dress well when they go out of the town. They can only be seen at their best in such places as the Promenade at Cheltenham. If this is true, it's rather unfair. Why shouldn't they try to brighten the streets of their own town?

This state of affairs was vividly illustrated to us a short time ago when we caught a glimpse of a really well-dressed woman in Bridge-street. She wore a form-fitting, tailor-made black outfit, with hat to match, and carried a tightly-rolled umbrella, which she seemed to be using as a walking stick. Her carriage and appearance were so striking that people turned to stare at her. A few girls giggled. But surely there must have been some glances of admiration apart from the men's?

Most Evesham men dress shabbily through necessity rather than through lack of taste. Market gardening is not a job for good clothes. The land takes a heavy toll in frayed cuffs, oily trousers and holey socks. When the men do dress up there is a tendency towards uniformity in their choice of style. Corduroy caps were all the rage at one time. Then came the 'loud' waistcoats. Check caps and hacking jackets are still popular.

Politically Evesham people are lukewarm. Most of them seem to have an unswerving devotion to their own particular party and a condescending attitude towards the opposition. There has not been a really rowdy political meeting for many years. The same applies to trade unionism. It is unlikely that Evesham will ever be featured in the news as a strike centre, in the true sense of the title, coupled with the fact that the main industry is broken up into small scattered units.

Summing up, we can say that the inhabitants of Evesham have nothing to be ashamed of in their character. There are very few real intellectuals, but there is a lot of sound common sense to make up for the lack. We may be cabbages, but our hearts are good.

9 780955 848711